THE FLEET HISTORIES SERIES
Volume III

The
REISS, PEAVEY, GARTLAND, FARRAR, WESTERN, BASSETT and FOOTE Fleets

Third Book in the Series
by
John O. Greenwood

A Historical Narrative and Photographic Depiction of Former and Present Great Lakes Fleets

Published by
FRESHWATER PRESS, INC.
1700 E. 13th Street, Suite 3-R
Cleveland, Ohio 44114

OTHER PUBLICATIONS OF FRESHWATER PRESS, INC.

Greenwood's Guide to Great Lakes Shipping (Annual)
Greenwood's & Dills' Lake Boats (Annual)
The Lakeboats Calendar
Namesakes 1900 - 1909 - John O. Greenwood
Namesakes 1910 - 1919 - John O. Greenwood
Namesakes 1920 - 1929 - John O. Greenwood
Namesakes 1930 - 1955 - John O. Greenwood
Namesakes 1956 - 1980 - John O. Greenwood
Namesakes of The 90's - John O. Greenwood
Fleet Histories Series-Volume I - John O. Greenwood
Fleet Histories Series-Volume II - John O. Greenwood
The Ford Fleet - C. J. Snider & M. W. Davis
Great Lakes Ships We Remember - Detroit Marine Historical Society
Great Lakes Ships We Remember II - Detroit Marine Historical Society
Great Lakes Ships We Remember III - Detroit Marine Historical Society
Lore of The Lakes - Dana Thomas Bowen
Memories of the Lakes - Dana Thomas Bowen
Shipwrecks of the Lakes - Dana Thomas Bowen
Ghost Ships of the Great Lakes - Dwight Boyer
Great Stories of the Great Lakes - Dwight Boyer
True Tales of the Great Lakes - Dwight Boyer
Ships and Men of the Great Lakes - Dwight Boyer
Strange Adventures of the Great Lakes - Dwight Boyer
The Lower St. Lawrence - Ivan S. Brookes
The Honorable Peter White - Ralph Williams
Great Lakes Fleet Identification Chart
Over 600 Photographs

**** Current Catalog Available Upon Request ****

© Copyright 1995 Freshwater Press, Inc.
Library of Congress Catalog No. 95-060635
ISBN: 0912514-33-7

Printed and Manufactured in the United States of America

**This book is dedicated to a good friend and fellow historian ---
the late Duff Gordon Brace.**

Duff was born in Conneaut, Ohio on April 2, 1914 and graduated from Conneaut High School in 1932. His childhood proximity to Conneaut's busy port spawned a life long interest in ships and railroads. Duff sailed on Great Lakes vessels as a porter, deckhand, and, finally, as a wheelsman on the Motor Vessel STEELMOTOR. He was drafted March 5, 1941 and spent five years in the U.S. Army Signal Corps. Following military service, Duff worked for eleven years at the Ashtabula & Buffalo ("A&B") Dock Company in Ashtabula, Ohio. He retired from the Sanborn Motor Equipment Company in 1980.

He was one of four local gentlemen who founded the Ashtabula Marine Museum in 1984 and he continued his active participation in that group until his death on August 5, 1995.

Duff married Jane Kelley on July 22, 1941. The couple has three daughters and four grandsons. It is with great pleasure that I recognize the valuable contributions to the Great Lakes shipping history preservation of Duff's efforts.

The couple is shown in April 1991 after Duff received the "Historian of the Year" award from the Marine Historical Society of Detroit.

John O. Greenwood

EXPLANATION & PREFACE

This book follows upon the overwhelming acceptance of the historical-photobiographical "NAMESAKES" Series of books on Great Lakes shipping and Volumes I & II of the "FLEET HISTORIES Series." This third volume describes company histories and provides totally different vessel photographs than those in either Volumes I or II.

It is intended that both United States and Canadian Great Lakes fleets will be included in the series. In some cases, ownership/management was interlocking between the two countries in one fleet operation. In other cases, all ownership was confined to one country or one general region.

Unless a fleet had, or has, such an extensive historical record, or voluminous fleet detail as to command a book of its own, several fleets are planned to be included in each book. These would be those fleets which, in general, have logical thread of connection with one another. Such is the case for fleets and vessels in the first three volumes.

In this volume, the Reiss, Peavey, Gartland, Farrar, Western, Bassett and Foote fleets are detailed. Early beginnings, fleet composition through the years, interesting sidelight facts, accident details, interesting incidents in the vessels careers and known management rationale for the rise and eventual cessation of operations are provided.

It is Freshwater Press' intent that readers will continue to enjoy this series and therein find many details and vessel photographs heretofore never before published.

Special thanks for assistance in the preparation of this volume, in alphabetical order, go to:
American Bureau of Shipping, George Ayoub, (late) J. H. Bascom, Jay Bascom, Duff G. Brace, Frank Braynard, (late) Milton J. Brown, Dossin Great Lakes Museum, Institute for Great Lakes Research, (late) James M. Kidd, Milwaukee Public Library, National Archives of Canada, William A. Reiss III, Arthur C. Sullivan, Jr., Fr. Peter J. Van der Linden and (late) Peter B. Worden.

It is with pleasure that we offer this Volume Three in the "Fleet Histories" Series.

John O. Greenwood

INTRODUCTION

The following **HISTORY OF THE IRON ORE TRADE** first appeared in the 1910 Lake Carriers' Association Annual Report and is restated here to provide a flavor of the genesis of the modern lake freighters that form a large part of the topics of this series of books.

"The iron ore trade is, of course, the great trade of the lakes, but it was not always so. The premier trade for so many years was grain, then lumber took first place, giving way subsequently to coal. In fact, it was not until 1888 that iron ore became the dominant trade of the Great Lakes. Its beginnings were very humble indeed. In order that future generations may have a historical reference, this article will trace the growth of the iron ore trade from its infancy to the present time. The iron ore trade had an influence upon the depth of the channels and gradual evolution in the type of steamer construction, through the development of loading and unloading appliances. The supremacy of our nation in the iron and steel trade of the world is more surely to be traced to the abundance of our Lake Superior ores and the low cost of their transportation on the lakes than to all of the tariffs ever written. The history of the trade is therefore, one of absorbing interest.

Iron ore was discovered on the Marquette Range on September 19, 1844 by William A. Burt, United States Deputy Surveyor, and a party who were surveying in the Upper Peninsula of Michigan. Burt was the inventor of the solar compass and it was the remarkable variations in the direction of the needle that caused him to ask his party to seek about for that which disturbed it. Outcroppings of ore were found in great abundance; in fact, a mere rip of sod revealed the ore.

In the spring of the following year, Philo M. Everett of Jackson, Michigan visited the region and discovered a deposit which he called the Jackson Mine. He returned to Jackson with a little of the ore, which was smelted. This was the first ore to leave the peninsula of Michigan. In the spring of 1846 a little house was built upon the Jackson Mine location, and when the party returned to Jackson, they carried about 300 pounds of ore on their backs. Some of the ore was taken to Mr. Olds of Cucush Prairie, who succeeded in making a bar of iron from it in a blacksmith's fire. This was the first iron ever to be made from Lake Superior ore. The next step in development was the construction of a forge on Carp River, about three miles from the Jackson Mine, and on February 10, 1848, the first iron from the Lake Superior region was made in this forge by Ariel N. Barney. The iron so made was sold to E. B. Ward who used it in the walking beam of the Steamer OCEAN. The forge had four fires, from each of which a lump was taken every six hours, which was placed under the hammer and forged into blooms 4 inches square and 2 feet in length, the daily product being about six tons.

The second forge was established by the Marquette Iron Company at the mouth of the Carp River in the spring of 1850. It received its ore from a mine later known as the Cleveland Mine, located about two miles from the Jackson Mine. The Jackson Mine was located at what is now known as Negaunee and the Cleveland Mine at what is now known as Ishpeming.

During the winter of 1850 about 25 double teams were employed in hauling ore to the forge at the mouth of the Carp River, where it was crushed and then made into bloom iron ready for shipment. The ore was hauled exclusively in sleighs during the winter. The attempt to make iron in the peninsula in these little forges proved most disastrous. The tedious hauling of the ore to the lake, the long carriage to the mills in Pennsylvania and Ohio made the cost of the bloom so expensive that it was impossible for the enterprise to recover its costs. By the time the blooms were laid down in Pittsburgh, they had actually cost $200.00 per ton, and the market rate for iron was then $80.00 per ton!

None of the early companies had any thought of shipping the ore itself to the lower lakes, though in 1850, Alexander Crawford of New Castle, Pennsylvania, had ordered ten tons of the ore sent to New Castle for testing purposes. Part of this ore was used by Mr. Crawford for puddler's fix in his rolling mill at New Castle. The mill was operated by the Cusola Iron Company. The balance of the ore was used in Wick's rolling mill at Youngstown, Ohio for the same purpose. In both cases, the ore was found to be quite satisfactory. It was not until 1853 that the iron companies concluded that the attempt to make iron in the upper peninsula was futile. They then took up the shipping of the iron ore to the lower lakes.

The beginnings of what has since become one of the greatest single trades in the world were certainly not impressive. It has been shown that the only method of bringing iron ore to the lake from the mines was by means of sleighs in the winter time. It became quite apparent that if any considerable business was to be done, the means of transportation would have to be improved. The average load of the sleigh was 3,000 pounds, or a little more than one and one-half gross tons, and was impossible for a team to make more than one trip a day. The whole winter's haul rarely exceeded 1,000 tons. This meant, of course, that no more than 1,000 tons could be shipped the following season.

Among the men attracted to the peninsula was Herman B. Ely, who as soon as he saw the deposits, recognized the need for a railway. He obtained the cooperation of the mining companies, but met with a cold response from capital sources elsewhere. The two mining companies then in existence waited patiently for a year for Mr. Ely to begin construction of his railroad, and then perceiving no sign of movement on his part, engaged jointly in the construction of a plank road to the mines.

The first shipment of ore in any quantity consisted of 152 tons, which was sent by the Cleveland Iron Mining Company to the Sharon Iron Company in Sharon, Pennsylvania in September, 1853. It took four vessels to move the ore from Marquette to Sault Ste. Marie, where it was portaged over the falls to be reloaded on another vessel. It was delivered to Erie, Pennsylvania and sent by canal boats to Sharon. The first boat load was delivered to the Sharpsville furnace.

The vessels on Lake Superior at that time consisted of three or four schooners ranging from 15 to 20 tons burden, and a couple of small steamers, all of which had been hauled over the portage at Sault Ste. Marie. Meanwhile, Congress had authorized a grant of land and a company known as the St. Marys Falls Ship Canal Company was organized to build a canal around the rapids at Sault Ste. Marie, Michigan. Mr. Erastus Corning, of Albany, New York, was president of this new firm. Actual construction work was begun in 1852.

Meanwhile, also, the two iron companies were working on their plank railroad and Herman Ely, who by now had been somewhat successful in raising some capital, was busily at work on building his railway. In the interim, ore was being hauled in sleighs as had been the practice. The tariff for the haul from the mine to the lake was $3.00 per ton and the price of the ore on the dock at Marquette was $8.00 per ton. The cost of mining was $.50 per ton which allowed a handsome profit if any good volume could be done.

Nearly the whole of the 1,000 tons of the ore on the dock when navigation opened in the 1854 was taken by the Forest City Iron Company. It was wheeled aboard the Steamers SAM WARD, NAPOLEON and PENINSULA in barrels and dumped upon the deck. At Sault Ste. Marie, it had to be unloaded and carried over the portage where it was again wheeled upon the vessels and taken to the lower lakes. In this business of portage it may be said in passing that Sheldon McKnight and his old gray horse and French cart occupy a picturesque and commanding position. The faithful animal had the honor in 1845 of hauling every pound of freight that passed to and from Lake Superior!

The canal at Sault Ste. Marie was opened on June 18, 1855, but it was not until November 1, 1855 that the plank railroad was completed to the mines. It lived a strenuous life for two years. The motive power was mules and the cars held about four tons each. A team could not make more than one trip a day, sometimes not even that, and for the entire motive power to move 35 tons from the mines to the lake was counted a big day's work.

When the Land Grant Act was passed in 1856, the plank railroad made overtures for consolidation with Ely's steam railroad. At this juncture Herman B. Ely suddenly died in Marquette, but work which he had undertaken was assumed by his brother, Samuel P. Ely. The steam railroad was finished to the mines in September, 1857. The locomotive Sebastopol was the first locomotive to be used on this railway and therefore the first in the iron country. It had been built by the New Jersey Machine & Locomotive Works of Paterson, New Jersey and was carried to Marquette on the deck of the Brig COLUMBIA in 1856. The same brig had carried the first cargo of iron ore from Marquette through the canal on August 17, 1855. Its cargo consisted of 132 tons consigned to the Cleveland Iron

Mining Company of Cleveland, Ohio. In all, 1,447 tons were shipped through the canal its first year of operation. The little dock at Marquette was a flat structure without trestle work, and the vessels were loaded by means of wheelbarrows. The crews of the vessels loaded the ore, being paid for doing so at the rate of $.25 per hour.

Practically all the shipments during the first few years were carried by schooners. All steamers in those days carried passengers and were ill-fitted to carry iron ore, though they would occasionally carry a deck load. As a rule the steamers avoided this freight if they could. Such a vessel as a bulk freighter had not been thought of. It was many years thereafter before the ore trade assumed any considerable volume. It had reached 114,401 tons in 1860, but fell to 49,909 tons in 1861, the slump being caused by the breaking out of the Civil War. The grain trade was then, and continued for many years thereafter to be, the premier trade of the lakes. For instance, the grain receipts at the port of Buffalo, New York alone in 1866 were about 1,500,000 tons, and the lumber receipts at Chicago, Illinois were about 400,000 tons, whereas the receipts of iron ore at all Lake Erie ports amounted to only 278,976 gross tons.

At this time, dimensions of the locks at Sault Ste. Marie were 350 feet long by 70 feet wide, with a depth over the sills of 11 feet six inches. This, of course, regulated the draft of vessels in Lake Superior service.

It was not until 1862 that any of the iron companies were sufficiently prosperous to justify the declaration of a dividend. Meanwhile, they had joined in building a wooden deck dock with trestle work at Marquette. The dock had pockets to facilitate the loading of iron ore. This facility was a primitive structure, but it was nevertheless a forerunner of the present great docks, embodying the principle of loading through a spout from a pocket.

Only schooners could be loaded with iron ore directly from the new dock's spouts because the steamers of the day were not yet adapted to the haulage of bulk cargoes such as iron ore. They did not have hatches through their decks, but gangways through the sides after the manner of the package freighters some forty to fifty years later, and beyond. Iron ore shipments to be moved by these early steamers was spouted on the dock and then wheeled aboard in barrows through the gangways. Schooners, therefore, pulled up on one side of the dock directly under the pockets and received their cargoes directly, while steamers moored on the opposite side of the dock. This side of the dock was flat-surfaced and capable of handling all classes of freight.

While the putting of iron ore aboard a schooner was comparatively a simple process even in those early days, getting it out again on the lower lakes was quite a different matter. The average cargo was about 300 tons and it took nearly four days to unload it. First of all, a staging had to be built in the vessel's hold upon which the cargo was shoveled, to be re-shoveled upon the deck and then loaded into wheelbarrows and wheeled to the dock. An improvement upon this practice was to unload by means of block, tackle and horse.

The firm of Bothwell & Morris, who operated the NYPANO dock in the Old River Bed at Cleveland, Ohio usually employed about forty horses in the work of unloading a schooner. One day in the spring of 1867, J. D. Bothwell, who was watching a small engine lifting piles into the air preparatory to driving them into the river bed, conceived the idea that an engine of somewhat similar design could also hoist iron ore from the hold of a vessel. He approached Robert Wallace, of Pankhurst & Company with the idea, and Wallace at once designed and built a little portable 6' X 12' engine fastened to the side of a boiler. It could be moved along the dock to any desired location. After the engine had been installed the first vessel to come along was the Bark MASSILLON. The little engine proved to be much more expeditious in its work than the horses, unloading the bark in a single working day. The engine operated three strands of rope fall, hoisting from the hold of the boat three tubs of iron ore at a time. Orders were given immediately for nine of these little engines and they proved very profitable to the firm of Bothwell & Morris, as their contract with the railway was based upon a fixed percentage of the tonnage handled.

It was the usual practice at this time for schooners to be towed through the rivers, in which business a large number of tugs found profitable employment. In the early 1860's, 93 per cent of the tonnage on the lakes was sail and less than 7 per cent was steam. This led to the construction and operation of a large fleet of tugs on the Great Lakes. A total of about fifty tugs were employed in various Great Lakes ports. Among these vessels were a number of the most powerful and fastest tugs in the world at that time, some of them towing as many as eight to ten schooners in a single *tow.*

In the early 1870's steam superseded sail so rapidly that the necessity for tugs very rapidly decreased, until the necessity of them for vessel towing purposes ceased to exist.

This method of transportation may be said in general terms to have been the method of the '60's. It was superseded in the early '70's by the system of steamer and barge/barges. In 1869 appeared the forerunner of the then-present type. The Steamer R. J. HACKETT was built by Peck & Masters Shipyard at Cleveland, Ohio, during that year to carry the ore from the Jackson Mine. As the term is now understood, she was the first bulk freighter to be built on the lakes. The HACKETT was 225' in overall length and 32' in width. The engine was mounted in the after cabin. In 1870, the same yard produced the Schooner FOREST CITY, measuring 221' in overall length and 33'6" in width. This vessel was towed in iron ore service by the HACKETT. This system of iron ore transportation by steamer and consort grew rapidly. In fact, it may be said to have been the prevailing practice for twenty years thereafter.

In 1874, the Steamer V. H. KETCHAM was built at the David Lester Shipyard in Marine City, Michigan. Thousands gathered to see her launched on April 16th for this carrier was twenty feet longer than anything afloat and was regarded as a "monster." She was, in fact, far in advance of dock facilities, though she later became very profitable. The KETCHAM's dimensions were: 242' in overall length, 41' in beam and 24' in moulded depth.

As previously noted, the draft of iron ore vessels was regulated by the depth of water in the locks at Sault Ste. Marie. By 1870 vessels drawing 13 feet and upward could enter a few of the more important ports, such as Buffalo, New York, Cleveland, Ohio and Chicago, Illinois. The demand became general for a depth of 16 feet throughout the Great Lakes system. The initiative to accomplish this was taken at the St. Marys Falls Canal by a project to increase its depth from 12 feet to 16 feet by building a new lock that would be 515 feet long and 80 feet wide, overcoming the difference of level of 18 feet between Lakes Superior and Huron by a single lift. The original locks were tandem, having a lift of 9 feet each. The new lock was completed in 1881, but the 16-foot channel in the rivers was not completed until 1884. Meanwhile, the principal harbors had been put in readiness and a fleet of large vessels built to take advantage of the new allowable draft. Iron ore shipments had increased from 278,796 gross tons in 1866 to 2,518,693 gross tons in 1884. The number of vessels had increased but slightly, but the gross registered tonnage had increased about 50 per cent. The freight rate on iron ore, which had fluctuated from $3.00 to $6.00 per gross ton in 1866, had fallen to $1.35 per gross ton in 1884.

In 1882 a departure from the use of wood as a shipbuilding material was made by the construction of the Steamer ONOKO at the Globe Iron Works in Cleveland, Ohio. That vessel was made of iron. The ONOKO measured 302'6" in overall length, 38'6" in breadth and 24'8" in moulded depth. For a time it was the largest dead-weight carrier on the lakes and was the first metal bulk freighter constructed on the Great Lakes. The first steel bulk freighter made its appearance on the lakes in 1886. This was the Steamer SPOKANE which was built for the Wilson Transit Company at the yard of the Globe Iron Works, Cleveland, Ohio. This steamer was 324' in overall length, 38' in beam and 24' in moulded depth.

It was not until 1888 that iron ore became the leading article of freight on the Great Lakes. During that year, 5,063,877 gross tons were moved. The growth in vessel tonnage had been steady though cautious. When the 16-foot channel was first projected, the tonnage varied from 600 to 1,000 tons net register, with a carrying capacity about twice the registered tonnage. When the 16-foot channel became available in 1881, the tonnage had grown from 1,500 to 1,900 net register, with a carrying capacity about double that, the increase in size being most marked in steam vessels.

In construction features the type of vessel had practically not varied from the design of the HACKETT and FOREST CITY, except that they were somewhat larger. In 1889, however, the first of a new type appeared, known as the whaleback. These vessels were commonly called "pigs," which, when fully laden, they greatly resembled. This design of vessel was conceived by Alexander McDougall of Duluth, Minnesota. The first such craft was called NO. 101 when launched. It was 198' in overall length, 25' in beam and 18' in moulded depth. This class of carrier created *quite a furor for the time being and many thought the type would revolutionize the type of bulk freighter on the lakes because within three years some 30 of them were built. The vessels were normally operated in fleets, that is, one steamer towed one or more barges. The whalebacks were economical to construct and were great carriers, but experience proved that their advantages did not surmount their disadvantages and this type vessel was gradually discarded in the iron ore trade. One by one, and sometimes in groups, these vessels largely disappeared, with only about a half dozen left on the lakes in 1910. It has been the history of lake practice than an improvement is no sooner completed than it is found to be totally inadequate to the demands of commerce. The 16-foot channel was no sooner completed when it was realized that it could not permanently care for the growth of lake shipping. Steps were immediately taken to establish a draft of 20 feet.*

The construction of a new lock at Sault Ste. Marie was undertaken under the direction of General Orlando M. Poe and a new channel was opened through the system of small lakes and straits known as the St. Marys River, saving eleven miles in distance and practicable for night navigation. In fact, the extent of the improvements in the connecting channels of the lakes is not generally realized. Between Lakes Superior and Huron the aggregate length of new or deepened channels is about 25 miles. Between Lakes Huron and Erie it is about 23 miles. The great commerce of the lakes, therefore, passes through an artificial waterway of 48 miles. This is 12 miles greater than the length or restricted waterway to be made at the Panama Canal. The new lock, known as the Poe Lock, was built upon the site of the original locks completed in 1855. The Poe was opened to traffic in 1896.

As indicating the influence of this gateway into Lake Superior upon vessel construction, it may be noted that more than half the tonnage of bulk freighters built in 1896 exceeded 2,000 tons net register. Six years before, not a single vessel of this tonnage was in service, the mean dimensions of freighters even as late as 1894 being under 300 feet.

In 1895 the first of the 400-footers appeared. This was the Steamer VICTORY, designed and built by the Chicago Shipbuilding Company at Chicago, Illinois under the direction of W. J. Babcock. The VICTORY measured 400' in overall length, 48' in beam and 28' in moulded depth. It was capable of carrying 5,200 gross tons of iron ore at an 18-foot draft. This vessel was taken as an example of the highest development of the bulk freighter at that time. The conditions required for lakes bulk freight movements on the Great Lakes lent themselves to open cargo holds, unobstructed by middle decks. The main deck beams of the VICTORY were uniformly spaced eight feet apart, making a beam at the end of the hatch and one in the center between hatches, the hatches through the upper or spar deck being 8 feet fore and aft and 24 feet between centers.

It is impossible to intelligently trace the growth of the lake freighter without noting the coincident development of the unloading machine, for the type of unloading machine has virtually dictated the type of steamer. As late as 1880, all vessels were being unloaded by wheelbarrows, little engines on the dock as noted previously, hoisting the buckets out of the hold. In 1880, however, Alexander E. Brown, a young man of great inventive faculties, employed in the office of his father, Fayette Brown, one of the pioneers of the development of the iron ore country, turned his attention to the problem of unloading ships. He developed a single cable-wired rig which served the combined purpose of hoisting the bucket from the hold and conveying it to storage. This rig was installed on the N. Y. P. & O. dock at Cleveland, Ohio in 1882. The plant as installed consisted of five rigs with machinery all in one house. The front pier of these machines was movable, and they were the first movable pier cableways ever built in the United States. They reduced the time of unloading remarkably, but naturally, as the tubs were small and had to be filled by hand, large hourly capacities could not be obtained. But, as the ore could be taken from a number of hatches simultaneously by the rigs, the time of total unloading was greatly reduced.

It is curious that the next step in the development of vessel tonnage should have been made by an interest quite alien to the lakes and without experience in ship owning, ship building or ship operating. During the financial panic of 1893, John D. Rockefeller had become, quite accidentally perhaps, the owner of several iron ore deposits in the Lake Superior region. He contracted the mines' output for delivery to the Carnegie Steel Company. To win a profit from the transaction and to take advantage of the steadily deepening channels, he gave orders through the Bessemer Steamship Company in 1897 for twelve Great Lakes vessels, some of them exceeding in dimensions those of any existing vessel. The largest of the dozen was 475' in length. Thanks to this order, more than half of all the steel tonnage built in the United States during that year was the product of lake shipyards.

It is interesting to note that this order from the Bessemer Steamship Company included two consorts 450 feet in length, though in the early 1890's the practice of building consorts began to be gradually abandoned. Vessel owners began to perceive that the highest economy of operation was reached by the single steamer of large carrying capacity and low power. There was justification of the consort system in the days of wooden ship building because a fleet of sailing ships was in existence whose natural destiny in the evolution of trade was that of a consort. It was not, however, economic to build a new steel vessel for consort purposes. No vessel owner would think of building a consort by 1910, and in fact, none have been built in the past thirteen years.

In 1899 George H. Hulett induced the Carnegie Steel Company to install on its docks at Conneaut, Ohio a new type of unloading machine operating a self-filling bucket. The introduction of a bucket that filled itself worked a revolution in lake practice and all the changes that have come about since have been to the end that the operation of this bucket might be facilitated. In fact, the Hulett unloading machines were unique to the Great Lakes. Over the years they established themselves as the fastest shoreside unloading equipment ever operated in the world!)

It was in 1900 that the first 500-footers appeared on the Great Lakes. During that year Augustus B. Wolvin commissioned four steamers to be built. The Steamers WILLIAM EDENBORN and ISAAC L. ELLWOOD were each 497' X 52' X 30' in overall dimensions and were built at the West Bay City Shipbuilding Company in West Bay City, Michigan. The Steamers JOHN W. GATES and JAMES J. HILL were of identical dimensions and were constructed at American Ship Building Company in Lorain, Ohio. The ships were called "500-footers" because their size approached that overall length so closely. This lead established by Captain Wolvin was not immediately followed, the tendency during the next several years being towards a somewhat smaller ship approximating 450 feet in length. The facilities afforded by the new dock facilities, however, were gradually working an evolution in the type of bulk freighter on the lakes.

As stated earlier, the ore pockets of the loading docks were spaced on 12-foot centers. With hatches spaced on 24-centers, the vessel could receive its cargo from every other pocket simultaneously. When that series of pockets emptied, the vessel would shift along the dock twelve feet to be exactly in line to receive ore from the alternate series of loaded pockets.

Captain Wolvin had the Steamer JAMES H. HOYT constructed in 1902 at the plant of the Superior Shipbuilding Company in West Superior, Wisconsin. This bulk freighter had hatches spaced on 12-foot centers which allowed it to receive iron ore from the spouts in every hatch simultaneously. The carrier had nineteen hatches and measured 376' in overall length, 50' in breadth and 27' in moulded depth. On her first trip, the HOYT took aboard 5,250 gross tons in the record-breaking time of 30.5 minutes and, upon arrival in Conneaut, Ohio, was unloaded in 3 hours and 52 minutes.

Two years later, Captain Wolvin made the most tremendous jump forward in ship size that had been made to date when he commissioned the American Ship Building Company to build, at its Lorain, Ohio yard, the Steamer AUGUSTUS B. WOLVIN. It was, in overall dimensions: 560' X 56' X 32'. The carrier also departed radically in constructive features from the common lake steamer of the day. Not only were her 33 hatches spaced upon 12-foot centers, but her hold construction was novel. Main deck beams and stanchions were omitted entirely and compensating strength was secured by a heavy plate girder, or arch, across the ship under the spar deck between every other hatch. These were connected to heavy plate webs running around the entire ship. The tank top was bent up to meet the main deck stringer in the form of a slope, thus forming a continuous hopper. This hopper contrivance not only increased the water ballast capacity of the ship, but brought the ore cargo completely within the sphere of the unloading machines. This form of construction gave total freedom from hold obstruction and allowed the unloading machines free play upon the cargo. Moreover, it permitted the ore pile to be concentrated upon a small bottom area and, therefore, steep and high, affording the utmost convenience to the self-loading buckets. The success of the WOLVIN was instantaneous.

On her maiden voyage, the WOLVIN loaded 10,694 net tons of iron ore at Two Harbors, Minnesota for delivery to Conneaut, Ohio. The cargo was discharged in 4 hours and 30 minutes by four Huletts and four Brown Hoists working jointly on the vessel.

Since the building of the WOLVIN, every vessel on the lakes has been built on the girder system, up through 1910. Some have girders straight, some are of arch form and some have hopper sides straight instead of sloping, or have no hopper at all, but none have been constructed on the old system of main deck beams and stanchions.

The old order of things entirely passed away. Old vessels were scrapped or altered or forced into other trades and vessel owners filled the shipyards with orders for vessels of this new type.

An example of the above was the order by the Pittsburgh Steamship Company. Through its president and general manager, Harry Coulby, the firm gave orders to the American Ship Building Company for four vessels to be nine feet longer than the WOLVIN. Subsidiary yards of the company built these freighters thusly: Chicago Shipbuilding Company, Chicago, Illinois - Steamers ELBERT H. GARY and WILLIAM E. COREY; West Bay City Shipbuilding Company, West Bay City, Michigan - Steamer HENRY C. FRICK and, Superior Shipbuilding Company, West Superior, Wisconsin - Steamer GEORGE W. PERKINS. Each vessel measured, in overall dimensions,: 569' X 56' X 31'.

Scarcely had the above four freighters been built before the same steamship company placed orders for eight more bulk freighters. All of these vessels measured 601' x 58' X 32' in overall dimensions except the Steamer THOMAS F. COLE which measured 605'6" X 58' X 32'. Five were built at Chicago Shipbuilding Company, Chicago, Illinois in 1906. These were the Steamers J. PIERPONT MORGAN, HENRY H. ROGERS, PETER A. B. WIDENER, THOMAS LYNCH and NORMAN B. REAM. The other three were built thusly: GEORGE F. BAKER at Superior Shipbuilding Company, HENRY PHIPPS at West Bay City Shipbuilding Company and THOMAS F. COLE at Great Lakes Engineering Works, Ecorse, Michigan. These latter four vessels began service in 1907.

Lake ship yards received a virtual avalanche of orders between 1904 and 1910, with vessel sizes ranging from 524' in overall length to the COLE AT 605'6". In 1905, 29 such bulk freighters were built; in 1906 - 40; in 1907 - 40; in 1908 - 24; in 1909 - 17 and in 1910 - 26.

Running expenses of these very large carriers were very little more than those of the older boats and they carried practically the same crew size. The engines also remained practically unchanged. The vessels built in 1888, carrying about 3,000 tons of ore, have the same machinery as the GARY, built in 1905, which is capable of carrying 10,000 tons of ore. In comparison to their size, these bulk freighters are obviously of very low power, but nevertheless sufficient for the purpose. The triple-expansion engine as installed on these ships has probably reduced economy to its least dimension, consuming 55-hundreths of an ounce of coal per ton mile carried.

As showing the great improvement in methods and cost of unloading, it may be stated that when vessels were unloaded by wheelbarrows it was estimated that it cost 50 cents per ton to unload them. When the first Brown hoisting and conveying machine was installed on the docks in Cleveland, Ohio, it was estimated that it had reduced the actual cost of unloading to 18 cents per ton, and there is every reason now to believe that the actual cost with the Huletts and modern clamshells does not exceed 5 cents per ton, if that.

In the general prosperity of the country, cheap transportation on the lakes has been a factor of prime importance. It is, in fact, responsible for the supremacy of the United States as an iron and steel making country. Were the waters of the lakes dried-up, no railroad, or system of railroads, could hope for a moment to handle this traffic. It would simply cease to exist. The great iron and steel plants of Ohio, Pennsylvania and the central west would close and thousands of allied industries would be abandoned. Three-quarters of all the ore used in the furnaces of the United States comes from the Lake Superior region. These deposits are one thousand miles away from the coke and limestone. Were it not for these Great Lakes, there would be no possible means of assembling the ore, coke and limestone to equal the furnace cost of those countries where the ore and coal lie in contiguous hills.

The rate per ton mile of moving freight on the Great Lakes during 1909 was .78 mills. A ton of iron ore is moved a thousand miles on the Great Lakes for seven-tenths of a mill per mile; a ton of iron ore is carried from Duluth, Minnesota to Buffalo, New York at a rate but little in excess of the ordinary railroad switching charge in any of the large cities.

The wonder of lake transportation is the suddenness of it, since it is but little more than half a century old, and its beginnings are well within the memory of men still living. Scarcely more than fifty years ago all the commerce of Lake Superior, as well as all the ships that carried that commerce, could be safely be stowed in the hold of any one of the steamers now engaged in that trade. Yet, there are so many vessels now employed in that trade that over a waterway of 1,000 miles one vessel is rarely out of sight of another.

The government is now engaged upon the construction of a third lock at Sault Ste. Marie to be 1,300 feet long and 80 feet wide. It is predicted that in the course of time a large portion of the rapids will be occupied by locks, and the time may be much sooner than expected, so rapid has been the expansion of lake trade. No plans have over-reached it; on the contrary, all have fallen far short in the works created to care for it."

R E I S S   S T E A M S H I P   C O M P A N Y
and its affiliated companies

The name Reiss has been associated with coal and Great Lakes shipping since well before the turn of the century. In modern times, before sale of the lake fleet in 1969, diversification into limestone, iron ore and other bulk commodities' carriage had come about through natural expansion.

Mr. Clemens Anthony Reiss, the firm's founder, was born November 7, 1835 in Croev, Germany on the River Mosel. He left his native country in 1855 for America to seek his fortune. After surviving a cholera attack in Chicago, Illinois, he moved to Two Rivers, Wisconsin and then to Sheboygan, Wisconsin to work for his future father-in-law as a baker. He spent the winter of 1856-57 working in the pine woods of Michigan, then returned to the Sheboygan area and worked in a flour mill at Pigeon River, saving enough from his wages to eventually purchase an interest in the mill. Mr. Reiss also bought property in Sheboygan and acquired part interests in Great Lakes schooners.

On May 10, 1864, Mr. Reiss married the daughter of his first employer - Miss Anna Mary Mallmann. She had been born on June 30, 1845 in Halsebach, Germany which was near Boppard on the Rhine River. Eight boys and four girls were born to this union and the establishment of the Reiss family involvement in Wisconsin affairs was assured.

Clemens Reiss established his coal business in 1880 as Clemens Reiss and Company with head-quarters in Sheboygan. Incorporation was formalized in 1888 as The C. Reiss Company, a name later changed to The C. Reiss Coal Company. Initial capitalization was established at $40,000.00. In a partnership arrangement with Messrs. Fritz Karste and Christian Eckhardt, Clemens Reiss held 18 of the firm's original 40 shares. His son Peter held 2 shares with Karste and Eckhardt each holding 10 shares. The Articles of Incorporation stated the purpose of the company was "selling and trading coal, wood, salt and building materials." While wood had ceased to be a product handled many years ago, the firm grew to handle many other materials such as pig iron, bentonite, coke, slag, stone and fuel oil.

Upon Clemens' death on June 5, 1896, Mr. Karste became president of the firm. He was succeeded in 1902 by Peter Reiss. Except for a few years during the 1970-1980 period, a Reiss family member continued to head The C. Reiss Coal Company.

Being located on the shore of Lake Michigan, and familiar with the great movements by water of both coal and lumber in the pre-1900 era, Clemens Reiss soon determined to get more heavily involved in Great Lakes transportation for his own account. As a result, the Steamer WILLIAM RUDOLPH and Schooner R. P. MASON were engaged under charter to carry coal, salt and pulpwood for the Reiss firm. This action took place in 1890. In 1895, the company purchased the bulk freight Steamer JOHN OADES from Mr. Aaron Adolph Parker of Detroit, Michigan. It, too, served in the same trades and was of wooden construction, the same as the two vessels that had been under charter. The OADES was not a long-term success, however, and it was sold to the Morton Salt Company in 1904. Both of these steamers had black hulls, white cabins and all black stacks.

On January 6, 1905 the Wisconsin Transportation Company was established as a Reiss subsidiary. Planning began for an enlarged fleet operation and, on June 6, 1905, the package freight Steamer AMERICA (2) and combination bulk and package freight Steamer BRAZIL were acquired. With this purchase the company retired their R. P. MASON and WILLIAM RUDOLPH as they were no longer required. They were sold to Messrs. Herman H. Pederson of Milwaukee, Wisconsin and Alfred F. Temple of Muskegon, Michi-

2

gan, respectively. The AMERICA (2) and BRAZIL also carried black hulls and white cabins, but their stacks held a C. Reiss Coal Company diamond logo on them with a white "R" centered inside the diamond. Other than this added detail, the stacks were solid black.

The Bulgaria Steamship Company was incorporated in Ohio on March 7, 1908 "to own and operate the wooden Steamer BULGARIA" with a capitalization of $25,000.00. The company purchased the vessel from Mr. Bernard Abraham of Sturgeon Bay, Wisconsin who had bought it at auction the previous year from Mr. James Corrigan of Cleveland, Ohio. The condition of the bulk freighter was not up to Reiss' expectations, however, and the vessel was sold in late 1909 to Mr. Frank W. Kerwanek of Denmark, Wisconsin. The BULGARIA's colors were the same as those of the OADES and RUDOLPH.

Another subsidiary was formed on December 28, 1909 in Charleston, West Virginia. This was the North American Steamship Company and it had a $350,000 capitalization. Its stated purpose in the Articles of Incorporation was "to operate vessels on the Great Lakes and to be in the general vessel business." Incorporators of the firm were: Messrs. Edward McBurney Byers - president of A. M. Byers & Company, Sylvester Kenworth Hine - president of the Girard Iron Company, John Dorchester Lyon - chairman of the Union National Bank of Pittsburgh, Fred Ignatius Kennedy - manager of the Cleveland, Ohio office of C. Reiss Coal and Roy Albert Williams - attorney. The latter gentleman had resigned his post with Pittsburgh Steamship Company to assume management of North American Steamship. Serving the new firm as its first president was Edward M. Byers, son of the late A. M. Byers.

North American vessels had white cabins, black hulls and all black stacks. When the navigation season opened in 1910, vessels under Reiss' management included: AMERICA (2), BRAZIL and three new vessels that would be delivered soon after the opening. These were the Steamer JOHN P. REISS, delivered on April 12th to Wisconsin Transportation and the Steamers A. M. BYERS, delivered June 16th and PETER REISS delivered July 5th to North American Steamship.

Management decided to merge Wisconsin Transportation and North American, with the latter being the surviving company, this action being finalized on December 31, 1912.

On March 20, 1916, four vessels were acquired from the Peavey Steamship Company for a net cash price of $250,000 each. These steel bulk freighters were purchased by the newly-formed Reiss Steamship Company of Minnesota which concurrently signed a long-term commitment with the F. H. Peavey Company of Minneapolis, Minnesota for the exclusive right and obligation to transport, or cause to be transported, all of that firm's domestic grain on the Great Lakes. The four vessels involved were: Steamers FRANK T. HEFFLEFINGER, FRANK H. PEAVEY, GEORGE W. PEAVEY and FREDERICK B. WELLS. The freighters were promptly renamed, respectively: CLEMENS A. REISS (1), WILLIAM A. REISS (1), RICHARD J. REISS (1) and OTTO M. REISS (1).

Shortly after the above-named acquisition, the Steamers AMERICA (2) and BRAZIL were sold, on March 27th, through Boland & Cornelius as brokers, to Mr. James Playfair of Midland, Ontario as these two ships had become excess capacity in the Reiss Fleet. Selling price was $125,000 per vessel.

On December 24, 1916, Reiss purchased the wooden Steamer ROUMANIA from Captain W. C. Richardson for $15,000.00. Due to its relatively poor condition, it was sold to D. Sullivan & Company on July 8, 1917 for the purpose of finding another buyer. D. Sullivan acted as intermediary in this instance and subsequently sold the hull to Captain William Nicholson of Ecorse, Michigan who intended to use the carrier as a barge.

2

Corporate operations were routine through World War I, but January 11, 1920 brought another set of mergings. That date, North American Steamship Company of Ohio (which had originally been incorporated in West Virginia) and Reiss Steamship Company of Minnesota merged to become the Reiss Steamship Company of Ohio with a capitalization of $750,000.00. Peter Reiss served as president and Captain James Doner was the fleet's manager.

On May 27, 1920, the Minnesota Transit Company was organized as a Reiss subsidiary with $260,000.00 in capital "for the purpose of purchasing the Steamers J. K. DIMMICK and W. K. BIXBY." These steel bulk freighters were acquired from the American Steamship Company of Detroit, Michigan, and National Steamship Company, also of Detroit, respectively. Both vessels were then renamed. The DIMMICK became the EDWARD U. DEMMER and the BIXBY became the J. L. REISS. The J. L. REISS remained in Minnesota Transit until March 6, 1921 when it was sold to Reiss Steamship Company. The DEMMER was sold in very early 1922 to the Milwaukee-Western Steamship Company, then managed by D. Sullivan & Company of Chicago, Illinois. These two transactions left Minnesota Transit Company without any floating assets. Minnesota Transit vessels were painted with black hulls, white cabins and all black stacks.

The Rockport Steamship Company was incorporated in Wilmington, Delaware on May 10, 1922 as a joint venture with the Cleveland Builders' Supply Company of Cleveland, Ohio. It had an original capitalization of $300,000.00 which was divided into 8,000 shares of no par common stock. The incorporators were: Messrs. William Anthony Reiss, John Adam Kling, James Doner and Peter Reiss. Each held one thousand shares at the time of incorporation with the balance held as Treasury Stock. The new company undertook to construct a self-unloading bulk freighter which was christened JOHN A. KLING in honor of the president of Cleveland Builders' Supply. This marked Reiss' initial entry into the arena of self-unloading lake carriers.

The year 1923 saw two additional acquisitions of second-hand tonnage when the Steamer JOSEPH W. SIMPSON was bought from the Milwaukee-Western Steamship Company and the Steamer ALEX B. UHRIG was purchased from the Mentor Transit Company. While the UHRIG remained in the Reiss Fleet until it was scrapped, the SIMPSON lasted only one season due to its small size and operating inefficiency. It was sold to Madden Coal Company of Ogdensburg, New York on August 16, 1924. Both vessels had been acquired on November 6, 1923.

The Reiss Steamship Company ordered and took delivery of a large bulk freighter in 1924 which it christened WILLIAM K. FIELD in honor of a personal friend of Peter Reiss, and the fact that he was an official of the Pittsburgh Coal Company. This was a firm which owned a 40% stake in The C. Reiss Coal Company in 1924. Success of Rockport's Steamer KLING led to the construction of another, larger self-unloading bulk vessel in 1925. The carrier had been planned originally to be a carferry, but those plans were changed in 1924 when the prospective customer changed its mind. The hull was completed as the Steamer CHARLES C. WEST. It became the first twin-screw bulk freighter on the Great Lakes.

More detail regarding the WEST is warranted. The hull design was actually very similar to other vessels being built at Manitowoc Shipbuilding which were twin-screw carferries with "cruiser" sterns. Reiss management was quite close to officials at the shipyard and knew of the plans for this hull and that these were not actually materializing with the proposed customer. Reiss investigated the possibilities of using the design for a self-unloader, especially one that could better serve one of its large customers, the White Pine Copper Company, which desired coal deliveries to the then unused port of Ontonagon, Michigan. The harbor was only reachable through a narrow, shallow channel and the only traffic had been lumber some years prior. Because the twin-screw design would allow the WEST to back out of the channel safely, Reiss officials decided to go forward with construction of the vessel. To further enhance the deal by the shipyard in Reiss' interest, the yard supplied two World War I surplus submarine engines that they owned at a "very

4

attractive" price. As negotiations progressed and were finalized, these engines were utilized and Mr. West's name was placed on the bow of the carrier.

The Rockport Steamship Company vessels were painted with black hulls, white cabins and fore-castles and had black stacks on which was mounted a large white "R."

A new Delaware corporation was established on March 13, 1925 which was named Reiss Steam-ship Company. It had capitalization of four million dollars. This was divided into 40,000 common shares without par value. Its original directors were: Messrs. W. A. Reiss - president and director, Clemens A. Reiss, Jr. - vice president and director, James Doner - treasurer and director, Omar D. Ballschmider - secre-tary and Peter Reiss and S. K. Hine - directors. This new concern combined all of the vessel ownerships and operations under one banner except for the joint venture Rockport Steamship Company, though it too, continued to be managed by Reiss.

An interesting "swap" of similar vessels occurred on April 8, 1926 between Reiss and D. Sullivan & Company, as managers of the Gartland Steamship and related fleets. This involved the Reiss Fleet trading their Steamer OTTO M. REISS (1) to the Chicago Navigation Company for the latter's Steamer JAMES S. DUNHAM. The swap came about because the DUNHAM had 9-foot hatch openings which were desirable for the coal trade and it was five years newer. On the other hand, the REISS was more powerful, had a carrying capacity about 8% greater than the DUNHAM and also consumed more fuel. The difference in the ships' respective values to their managements was made up by Reiss Steamship "throwing in" some of its shares to D. Sullivan & Company. Reiss renamed the carrier LYNFORD E. GEER.

Later in 1926, on September 4th, Peter Reiss died in Sheboygan Falls, Wisconsin. Upon his death, William A. Reiss was elected president of The C. Reiss Coal Company and all its subsidiaries. During the balance of the decade, the companies flourished, but were subject to the same shortfalls as most every other industrial-based concern during the early years of the Great Depression. The adage that "adversity breeds opportunity" proved correct when the Reiss Steamship Company decided to create its own self-unloading vessel. As noted earlier, the Reiss Fleet managed the two self-unloaders in the Rockport Steamship Com-pany. Their success led Reiss management to consider converting one of their bulk freighters into a self-unloader. The reconstruction contract was awarded to the Manitowoc Shipbuilding Company for conversion of the Steamer J. L. REISS to a self-unloader in 1933.

Following the constructive total loss of the Steamer WILLIAM A. REISS (1) on November 14, 1934 and the ship's sale for scrap, management sought a substitute carrier. The bulk freight Steamer JOHN A. TOPPING was purchased from the Columbia Transportation Company and was renamed WILLIAM A. REISS (2) to fulfill that need.

An essentially "private investment" company was incorporated in Delaware on February 8, 1937 with formation of the Red Arrow Steamship Company. The new firm was authorized to issue 2,000 shares of no par common stock. Only 400 of these were ever issued and capitalization was set at $100,000.00. The original officers were as follows: W. A. Reiss - president, C. A. Reiss, Jr. - vice president and Walborn Worthington Newcomet - secretary. Trusts set up by William A. Reiss through Red Arrow have benefited later generations of the Reiss family, and do so today.

Red Arrow Steamship Company Articles of Incorporation stipulated that shares could be sold only back to the Corporation and not to other individuals or organizations if any original shareholder wished to dispose of shares. The steamship company was more than a financial vehicle. It was the owner of the bulk freight Steamer JOE S. MORROW which it acquired from the Masaba Steamship Company in early 1937. This vessel was operated almost exclusively in the coal and grain trades its entire tenure in the management of the Reiss Fleet.

The MORROW and the balance of the Reiss Fleet of wholly-owned vessels carried black hulls, white cabins and forecastles with black stacks and a large white "R" mounted upon it. While the Reiss ships themselves also were painted with the Reiss diamond logo on their bows, the MORROW was not.

After the onset of World War II, the Reiss Steamship Company took delivery of the Steamer RICHARD J. REISS (2), a vessel which had been commissioned by the United States Maritime Administration. There were sixteen of these near-sister ships built for the Government's account and these were then sold to operating Great Lakes U. S. flag fleets for "traded-in" older tonnage, plus cash. In preparation for this 1943 addition, the Steamer RICHARD J. REISS (1) was renamed SUPERIOR (3) in 1943. This was one vessel "traded-in" to the Maritime Administration. The other was the venerable bulk freight Steamer ALEX B. UHRIG. After the end of the war, both carriers were sold for scrap.

The Reiss Fleet continued its modernization with conversion of the Steamers PETER REISS and A. M. BYERS to self-unloaders. The PETER was converted in 1949 and the BYERS in 1955.

In 1956, a joint venture was formed with the Gartland Steamship Company. The Redland Steamship Company was incorporated in Delaware on January 11, 1956 with one-half interest therein held by Gartland and the other one-half held by Red Arrow. Fuller corporate detail is provided in the Gartland story in this book because that firm was the actual manager of the steamer which was purchased and converted by Redland. The acquired ship was the bulk freight Steamer HENNEPIN (2) which was bought from the Cleveland-Cliffs Steamship Company in 1956. It was operated as a bulk freighter during the 1956 season while plans for its conversion to a self-unloader were negotiated and formalized. The conversion work was completed in 1957.

Upon the death of William A. Reiss, Sr. on October 24, 1959 in Chicago, Illinois, William A. Reiss, Jr. was elected chief executive of the Reiss Fleet. During the decade of the 1960's operations of the fleet were sustained, but there was also discussion of merger with other fleets as freight movements on the Great Lakes were on a plateau. One such discussion took place with the Tomlinson Fleet Corporation in 1963, but there was no conclusion towards accomplishment of the merger.

By vote of a majority of the board of directors on December 31, 1963, Rockport Steamship Company and Reiss Steamship Company were merged with Reiss being the surviving company. By mid-decade, there was some improvement in the fleet's prospects and management decided to purchase the bulk freight Steamer EMORY L. FORD from the Hanna Fleet. This action was closed on April 7, 1965 and the carrier was renamed RAYMOND H. REISS.

By later in the decade, however, with advent of 1,000-foot self-unloaders on the horizon, it seemed appropriate to Reiss management to consider getting out of the Great Lakes shipping business. Some "housekeeping" duties of the Red Arrow Steamship shareholders also appeared to be in order. Officers at the time were: William A. Reiss, Jr. - president, Jesse P. Feick - vice president, Robert T. Melzer - secretary and John H. Carpenter - treasurer. Of the then-outstanding 398 shares of Red Arrow, shareholders voted 383 "For" and 15 "Against" dissolution of the company. Such dissolution was effective as of June 27, 1969. The vote for this action was taken on June 4th.

The Reiss family was quite aware of their close associate's action in early March of 1969 when Gartland Steamship Company and its wholly-owned subsidiaries were sold to Oswego Shipping and became a subsidiary of American Steamship Company. Much thought was given to the matter, but shareholders approved the sale of all vessel assets of The C. Reiss Coal Company to American Steamship on June 27,

1969 for a price of $10,500,000.00. Integration of the fleets took place quickly and the Reiss Fleet's stack design, so long familiar on the Great Lakes, was stricken from those lakes. Under American, the Reiss Steamship Company continued to exist as a corporate entity until American's board approved its merger at a meeting on July 1, 1986. Following this vote, Reiss was merged into American on July 23, 1986.

Steamer WILLIAM RUDOLPH

This oak-hulled bulk freight vessel had a carrying capacity of 310,000 board feet of lumber and was a typical "lumber hooker" of its day. While in the Reiss Fleet, it is not known to have sustained any serious mishaps. Its namesake was Mr. William Rand Rudolph, the son of an early pioneer in the blue point oyster harvesting and merchandising business on the east coast. The senior Rudolph was instrumental in arranging financing for the carrier and a partner of Mr. James A. Prentice of Saginaw, Michigan who was the vessel's original owner.

Schooner R. P. MASON

Mr. Rufus Putnam Mason was this wooden schooner's namesake. He was prominent in the lumber business in Chesaning, Michigan as agent for Massachusetts financiers in the 1860's when this schooner was constructed. The vessel is not known to have had any accidents while serving in the Reiss Fleet.

Steamer JOHN OADES

This oak-hulled bulk freighter had a carrying capacity of 1,900 gross tons. It was built by John Oades and his son Walter, who owned a shipyard at the foot of Dubois Street in Detroit, Michigan. The yard built steamers, schooners and tugs. This vessel did not sustain any major mishaps while in the Reiss Fleet.

Steamer BRAZIL

The steel freighter BRAZIL had a cargo hold divided into three compartments whose total carrying capacity was 3,200 gross tons. The carrier served both as a package freighter and a bulk freighter since it had package freight space on the after part of the upper deck and main deck. Namesake of this vessel was the largest country in South America - Brazil.

During its years in the Reiss Fleet, the Steamer BRAZIL is only known to have sustained one costly accident. That occurred May 23, 1915 while the ship was drawing 19' 6" forward and 17' 3" aft. It was unusual to be drawing such water forward because it made the vessel more difficult to steer. Sailors refer to this condition as "being down by the head."

While passing downbound in the St. Clair River abreast the Idlewild Dock, and about three hundred feet from the Canadian side of the channel, the BRAZIL rubbed bottom forward and damaged fourteen bottom plates and internal framing. Ultimate cost of repairs came to $5,377.24.

Steamer AMERICA (2)

The steel package freight Steamer AMERICA (2) was named for the United States. During its service in the Reiss Fleet, it suffered only one recorded accident. That occurred on May 6, 1912 in the Straits of Mackinac. The carrier stranded while navigating in the vicinity of Waugoshance Shoal during dense fog. Serious bottom damage was sustained and it was later determined that Captain Arthur G. Tappan was proceeding at too fast a rate of speed. He was discharged by the Wisconsin Transportation Company for his error. Repairs to the ship were carried out at Manitowoc, Wisconsin with the bill totaling $11,986.55.

Steamer WILLIAM RUDOLPH in port when in the Reiss Fleet in 1902

Schooner R. P. MASON underway on Lake Michigan about 1912 after leaving the Reiss Fleet

8

Steamer JOHN OADES when in Reiss coal service about 1900.

Steamer BRAZIL while upbound with coal in the St. Clair River in 1914.

Steamer AMERICA (2) upbound at the Soo Locks in 1909

Steamer BULGARIA passing upbound above the Soo Locks in 1909

Steamer BULGARIA

This oak-hulled bulk freighter was only in the Reiss Fleet for the better part of two navigation seasons and had no recorded mishaps during that time period. It was named at its christening for one of the republics on the Balkan peninsula.

Steamer A. M. BYERS

The steel bulk freight Steamer A. M. BYERS was named posthumously in honor of Mr. Alexander McBurney Byers by his son, Edward, who was president of the firm of A. M. Byers and Company in 1910. The senior man had served as president of the wrought iron pipe manufacturing firm until his death in 1900. The carrier was equipped with a triple expansion engine which developed 1,760 shaft horsepower and two Scotch boilers with six furnaces. Steam pressure was 180 pounds per square inch.

While being operated in the Reiss Fleet as a straight deck bulk freighter, the BYERS suffered nine recorded accidents. Its most serious, however, occurred the year after it was converted to a self-unloader and will be discussed in some detail later in this chapter.

Detail of the nine recorded accidents follows:

1. September 11, 1913:
While passing upbound through Lime Kiln Crossing, Detroit River, at the upper gas buoy, the smoke from the dredge and drill boats working there obscured the lights and the BYERS went aground. Because of the rocky bottom in the river, repairs proved to be very expensive and totaled $41,489.69.

2. May 9, 1915:
The ship was making a landing at the Government Pier at the entrance to the new Davis Lock at the Soo Locks and was upbound. It struck the corner of the pier with its port bow, damaging several plates and frames. Cause of the accident was blamed on the changeable currents in the area by reason of emptying the lock chamber. Repairs were not costly and amounted to $1,494.50.

3. June 27, 1921, 0515 hours:
The BYERS was making a landing at the North Pier at the Soo Locks while the Davis Lock was being filled and the current caught the vessel and forced it over against the wooden stringer on the North Pier. This resulted in a dent to the vessel's port bow with repairs running to $2,715.65.

4. May 7, 1922, 2220 hours:
The vessel grounded in the draw of the railroad bridge at Green Bay, Wisconsin while drawing 18' 6" forward and 18' 4" aft. It was stated that the current in the Fox River was running eight miles per hour at the time and this condition forced the BYERS aground. Repairs to bottom plates and some framing came to $3,460.01.

5. June 21, 1922, 0645 hours:
During foggy weather and going upbound light, the BYERS weighed anchor from 0345 to 0630 hours in western Lake Erie below Detroit River Light. When the fog lifted the BYERS raised anchor and proceeded and passed three other boats to port when the fog suddenly set in again and obscured the view of four other following boats. This vessel was running under bare steerage way when the Steamer CRETE showed up out of the fog and the two carriers collided. Repairs were effected in the amount of $8,056.75 for both vessels.

6. June 25, 1922, 1445 hours:

While proceeding upbound in the St. Mary's River, at the Round Island Turn, the BYERS momentarily lost steering and collided with the downbound Steamer JAMES A. FARRELL. The BYERS suffered bow damage to the extent of $21,004.90 in repairs while port side damage to the FARRELL amounted to $32,868.09.

7. November 16, 1923:

During stormy weather and strong current flowing, the carrier grounded in Hay Lake, St. Mary's River, doing bottom plate and internal damage to the extent of $17,962.63 in repair cost.

8. November 5, 1925:

While bound from Escanaba, Michigan to Erie, Pennsylvania with iron ore, the vessel grounded at the lower end of Lake Huron on the Point Edward Ranges. Tugs freed the vessel and it proceeded to unload, then went into the Toledo shipyard for repairs which amounted to $17,879.94. Due to the lateness of the season, the carrier did not re-enter service.

9. July 27, 1935, 0900 hours:

Drawing 17' 3" all around and proceeding down Lake Erie, the propeller struck some obstruction 28 miles east-northeast of Long Point. The propeller was broken including the hub. The tail shaft was broken and the stern tube and outer bearings were damaged. Repair costs at Buffalo, New York totaled $21,087.09.

Steamer A. M. BYERS upbound with coal in Little Rapids Cut, St. Mary's River, as a bulk freighter in 1925.

Steamer JOHN P. REISS

The namesake of this bulk freighter was Mr. John Peter Reiss who was a vice president of The C. Reiss Coal Company in 1910 when this vessel took his name. The carrier was delivered by the building shipyard on April 12, 1910. It was equipped with a triple expansion engine and two Scotch boilers, each of which carried 180 pounds per square inch of pressure. The engine developed 1,760 shaft horsepower when operating at 83 revolutions per minute. The carrier had 12' hatches and straight side tanks which served to maximize cubic capacity in the holds for carriage of coal and grain.

During its tenure in the Reiss Fleet, this vessel sustained four major damages which are recorded below:

1. May 6, 1918:

While bound from Superior, Wisconsin to Cleveland, Ohio with iron ore, the ship encountered heavy ice in Lake Superior which resulted in corrugation of plates on both bows. Later repairs amounted to $8,683.16.

2. July 8, 1928, 0510 hours:

Light and while proceeding under slow speed in heavy fog and taking soundings with a lead line in the vicinity of South Manitou Island, Lake Michigan, the water shoaled up suddenly. Before the vessel was able to be stopped, she fetched up on what appeared to be a soft bottom. This was not exactly the case, however, as inspection on dry dock showed substantial bottom damage to plates and internal framing to the extent of $18,694.31 in repair cost.

3. November 10, 1930:

The steamer stranded near the Wyandotte Channel at Ballard's Reef in the lower Detroit River, damaging fifty-seven sideshell and bottom plates. At the time, the vessel was downbound with grain destined for delivery to Buffalo, New York. Number one tank flooded and the Lighter RELIANCE, along with Tugs HARDING and OREGON were called to assist. They brought air compressors to the scene and lightered about 20,000 bushels of wheat before freeing the vessel on November 12th. As it turned out upon hull inspection, many of the damaged plates did not require renewing. Thus, total repair cost was only $4,961.64.

4. May 15, 1933, 1730 hours:

With Captain E. J. Lawrence in command, the vessel was light coming up the Black Rock Channel from the Wickwire Steel Plant and met a tug with four Erie Canal barges in tow about 1,000 feet north of the Bird Island Light. The tug and tows crowded the REISS over against the channel bank where she received severe damage on her starboard bilge. Owing to the lack of much insurance on many of the canal craft in this time period, the REISS had to pay almost all of its damages even though it was not judged to be at fault. Total repair cost was $13,724.79.

Steamer JOHN P. REISS downbound in Little Rapids Cut, St. Mary's River during 1936.

Steamer PETER REISS

The Steamer PETER REISS honored a senior member of the Reiss family who was helpful in the steamship and railroad side of their coal business. His namesake was a carrier of 9,000 gross tons carrying capacity and largely served in the coal and limestone trades. The vessel sailed on its maiden voyage May 27, 1910 from Duluth, Minnesota with iron ore for delivery to Ashtabula, Ohio.

During its service in the Reiss Fleet, a total of seven accidents were recorded which could be considered of a major nature. These are as follows:

1. October 3, 1915:
The steamer was approaching the Allouez iron ore loading Dock No. 4 in the usual manner with the port anchor down. The wind and current was sufficient to carry the vessel over, striking the corner of the ore dock. Damage was done to the shell plating on the starboard bow and also to plates abreast No. 11 and 12 hatches. The repairs were carried out at Superior, Wisconsin at a cost of $6,380.78.

2. July 23, 1918:
The Steamers PETER REISS and GLENSHEE were in collision this date while the REISS was going into the west side of No. 3 ore dock at Duluth, Minnesota in tow of the Tug WISCONSIN. The weather was foggy and a large current was running in the St. Louis River. While recorded in insurance registers as a "casualty," the loss attributed to the REISS was but $962.76 for repair costs to the GLENSHEE. Its own costs of repair were much greater at $13,099.77.

3. October 5, 1925, 1030 hours:
While warming up its engine at No. 1 ore dock at Two Harbors, Minnesota, the wheel struck some obstruction, breaking the tail shaft. The wheel dropped off the vessel and lodged on the shoe of the rudder. The vessel was towed to the C. & P. Ore Dock in Cleveland, Ohio by the Steamer CLEMENS A. REISS (1) and, after being unloaded, was drydocked at American Ship Building's yard in Cleveland. There, repairs were effected to the cost of $10,166.42.

4. September 30, 1928, 0730 hours:
Approaching the Reiss Coal Dock in Superior, Wisconsin, and in backing to make the turn into the slip, the REISS backed to starboard due to the current setting in. This caused the port bow to come into collision with spring piling in a cluster which was at the end of the Berwind Coal Dock No. 1. Damage was done to two plates and internal framing with repair costs amounting to $2,662.57.

5. October 13, 1928:
The REISS grounded in the turning basin at the head of the Buffalo River in Buffalo, New York. Due to the rocky and shoaled bottom channel, repairs to damaged plates and frames was extensive and amounted to $23,321.68.

6. May 31, 1929, 2320 hours:
In making the turn to get through the piers at Milwaukee, Wisconsin, and meeting an incoming carferry, the REISS caught suction from the south channel bank. This caused the vessel to drift and the master reversed the engine promptly. Before headway could be stopped, however, the port bow came into collision with the North Pier. Port bow and minor internal structural damage came to $3,932.68 in ship repair costs.

7. August 4, 1935, 0835 hours:

Light and making a turn under the starboard helm while going into the Pennsylvania Railroad Coal Dock at Sandusky, Ohio, with wind light from the northwest, the vessel failed to respond to her helm.

This was said to be caused by the strong current setting in from the eastward. The bow fetched up against the northwest corner of the east dock, doing considerable damage to the port bow. Upon inspection, it was found necessary to make repairs at the cost of $11,550.63.

Steamer PETER REISS upbound with coal as a bulk freighter in Little Rapids Cut, St. Mary's River during 1925.

Steamer CLEMENS A. REISS (1)

This vessel was delivered to its original owner on October 20, 1901. It was equipped with a quadruple expansion engine of 1,700 shaft horsepower. It also had two Scotch boilers of 250 pounds per square inch pressure each and a loaded speed of 12 miles per hour.

Namesake of this carrier was Mr. Clemens Anthony Reiss, founder of the Reiss family enterprises. In its tenure in the Reiss Fleet, this vessel had three recorded accidents, which are as follows:

1. May 14, 1917:

In leaving the anchorage at Big Point, above the Soo Locks, for the Poe Lock, and when at a point abreast of Vidal Shoal, the vessel was ordered to stop by the Soo lockmaster's patrol boat. In attempting to turn around, the REISS stranded. There was damage to the ship's bottom and internal framing which involved $9,060.22 in repair cost.

2. July 1, 1918:

The REISS and the Steamer RICHLAND DAISY were in collision at the port of Ashtabula, Ohio due to the REISS swinging too far to port and striking the RICHLAND DAISY on the starboard quarter. Damage to the steel-hulled REISS was not noticeable, but that of the RICHLAND DAISY, being of wooden construction, cost the REISS $988.60 to repair.

3. August 20, 1927, 0650 hours:

The REISS was leaving the ore dock at Fairport, Ohio, with a tug to shove her out stern first into Lake Erie. When about 800 feet away from the breakwater light, the REISS began to sheer over towards the west breakwater and the stern collided with the crib, damaging plates and frames on the starboard quarter. Repairs cost $2,669.55.

Steamer CLEMENS A. REISS (1) passing downbound in the St. Mary's River during the 1927 navigation season.

Steamer OTTO M. REISS (1)

The steel bulk freight Steamer OTTO M. REISS (1) was equipped with a quadruple expansion engine which developed 1,700 shaft horsepower and two Scotch boilers which carried 250 pounds per square inch each. The typical loaded speed of the carrier was 12 miles per hour when consuming 3,400 pounds of coal per hour.

The namesake of this vessel was Mr. Otto Martin Reiss. Unfortunately, Otto was only a young man of twenty-five when he died following an operation for appendicitis on May 4, 1917 just as he was learning the business aspects of the Reiss family. His namesake is known to have suffered six different mishaps during its period of operation in the Reiss Fleet.

1. October 27, 1917:

The Steamers OTTO M. REISS (1) and MARY C. ELPHICKE collided in the harbor at Ashtabula, Ohio this date. The ELPHICKE's bulwarks were completely demolished for about twelve feet on her starboard quarter and her stern anchor table and winch compressor were broken. The stem of the REISS was badly dented, but was not otherwise damaged. The REISS' repair costs amounted to $4,165.41.

2. July 18, 1924, 1230 hours:

Drawing 19 feet all around, the vessel rubbed bottom at the head of Little Rapids Cut, St. Mary's River, while making the turn off the Bayfield Rock Range into the Cut. Repairs were extensive on the bottom and sideshell plates and internals supporting them. Repair costs amounted to $20,585.30.

3. May 6, 1925, 1530 hours:

In making a landing in the slip at Rockport, Michigan, the REISS sagged against the port bank where there existed jagged gravel and boulders. Damage was done to plating in way of No. 8 and 9 hatches below the waterline with repairs costing $7,056.21.

4. September 9, 1927:

This date the REISS and the Steamer S. B. WAY (1) collided in the dredged channel from Lake Erie into Maumee Bay, near Toledo, Ohio. At the time of this accident, the Tug NAVAGH was attending its dredge which was performing work in the channel. The Reiss Fleet claimed that the WAY had not gotten out of its path after the two ships exchanged passing signals. The WAY claimed that the REISS obstructed the channel necessary for the navigation of the WAY in the area the tug was working with the dredge anchored. The matter was submitted to arbitration for a decision of fault. Arbitrator Robert G. McCreary determined that the REISS was one-third at fault and the WAY two-thirds and that the Tug NAVAGH should be exonerated. The total costs involved in repairs of $22,566.98 were to be shared between the parties according to this formula of percentage of fault.

5. September 24, 1928:

Following discharge of an iron ore cargo, the REISS grounded on a rock shelf in the Calumet River in South Chicago, Illinois. Cause of the grounding was given as the swift current which was running in the river at the time. Damage to bottom plating amounted to $5,296.51 in repair costs.

6. November 21, 1928:

While being towed by the Tug KANSAS in the Calumet River at South Chicago, the REISS jammed its rudder and broke its shoe while backing away from a grain elevator slip. Before the extent of damage was discovered, the rudder fell off and was lost. Divers later found the rudder, but not for several weeks. Meanwhile, the REISS was drydocked in South Chicago and repairs were completed at a cost of $15,870.26.

Steamer OTTO M. REISS (1) in 1918 while downbound in Little Rapids Cut, St. Mary's River.

Steamer GEORGE W. PEAVEY

This 7,000 gross ton capacity bulk freighter only served in the Reiss Fleet under this name during the navigation season of 1916. Then it was renamed. Its namesake in 1916 was Mr. George

Wright Peavey, son of Mr. F. H. Peavey. He was with the Peavey Company, grain merchandisers and millers, until that firm was incorporated in 1906. At that time, he sold his interest in the firm to his two cousins and took up other pursuits. During 1916, the carrier was not involved in any mishaps.

Steamer RICHARD J. REISS (1)

This bulk freighter had four cargo compartments in its hold and a carrying capacity of 7,000 gross tons. It was named for Mr. Richard John Reiss who was but 34 years old when it took his name in 1916. He was then serving as manager of the St. Paul, Minnesota office of the company and appeared to have a bright future. Because of his health condition, however, he was forced to resign and move to Colorado early in his career. Climatic conditions were more healthful to him in that area.

During its tenure of service in the Reiss Fleet under this name, this carrier was known to have sustained five casualties which are enumerated below.

1. May 16, 1924, 0745 hours:
Drawing 15' 6" forward and aft, the vessel was proceeding up the river at Manitowoc, Wisconsin on its way to the plant of the Manitowoc Cement Company with a cargo of coal when it found dredges anchored in the channel about 1,000 feet from its destination. To navigate around this moored obstruction, the REISS was required to hold its starboard side to the opposite bank to avoid hitting the dredges. In so doing, the ship struck some other obstruction and rolled to port somewhat. Repairs at the local yard amounted to $11,222.49 for bilge and bottom plates and internal framing.

2. September 8, 1933, 1900 hours:
With Captain Thomas Moar in command, the REISS was proceeding into the iron ore loading dock, light, at Allouez, Wisconsin when it struck the end of the concrete dock head on. Cause of the accident was laid to both swift currents and the probable excess speed of approach of the REISS. Repair costs for stem and plating adjacent to it ran to $10,612.03. Since the vessel was dragging its anchor at the time, it became obvious to investigators that tugs should also have been used to more safely guide the REISS to its loading berth.

3. May 3, 1934, 0150 hours:
With Captain Moar again in command, the vessel was loaded with coal and bound for the company dock in Sheboygan, Wisconsin. Drawing 17' 9" forward and 17' 7" aft, it was entering the breakwater in the Sheboygan River with a northeast wind blowing and sea running. Steerage became difficult and the REISS rubbed bottom on the port side for its entire length. Temporarily low water and squat of the vessel was blamed for the accident. Upon examination in drydock at Manitowoc, Wisconsin, it was found that plates were damaged from bilge to bilge, and rivets were leaking or missing in the rudder shoe and stern post and that the vessel was damaged for practically the entire length of its keel. Repairs of $27,828.65 were required and the company dismissed Captain Moar from his command.

4. November 23, 1934, 0800 hours:
The REISS had loaded a cargo of bituminous coal at Sandusky, Ohio and was departing for Milwaukee, Wisconsin when it stranded at the harbor entrance.. A large hole was punched in the bow and six feet of water was taken in the forepeak and in cargo hold #1. The vessel had to be lightered of some of its coal to be refloated. Following lightering 420 net tons of coal, the ship was released and towed to drydock at Lorain, Ohio for repairs costing $19,904.40 before it was able to continue on to deliver its cargo to Milwaukee.

18

5. October 5, 1935, 2200 hours:

The carrier collided with the Steamer CARLE C. CONWAY while both vessels were at anchor during a storm which was occurring above the Soo Locks in the upper St. Mary's River. The wind changed direction suddenly and the CONWAY's bow swept around and rammed the REISS, punching a large hole in the REISS' bow. Damage to the REISS was confined to the port bow and forepeak and she was allowed to transit to Superior, Wisconsin when the storm subsided to be unloaded of its coal cargo. It was then drydocked in Superior where repairs were made which totaled $18,864.05.

Steamer GEORGE W. PEAVEY downbound below the Soo Locks in 1916

Steamer RICHARD J. REISS (1) passing upbound with coal in the Detroit River during the 1940 navigation season.

Fleet Histories Series III

Steamer WILLIAM A. REISS (1)

Mr. William Anthony Reiss was this bulk freighter's namesake. He was a vice president of The C. Reiss Coal Company in 1916 when this carrier took his name. It was a ship of 7,000 gross tons carrying capacity and is known to have sustained three damaging accidents prior to the one that ended its career in 1934. All four are noted below.

1. May 11, 1920, 0700 hours:

While entering the harbor at Huron, Ohio, and directly in the channel about a boat's length from the entrance, this vessel was caught by undertow and was carried towards the west pier where it struck wooden stringers on the corner of the pier. Damage was done to the starboard plates which required repairs in the amount of $4,823.91.

2. October 12, 1927, 0716 hours:

Drawing 18' 7" forward and 19' 4" aft, the REISS grounded on Southeast Shoal during dense fog, damaging six bottom plates and some internal framing. The carrier was upbound with coal at the time, but was able to free itself when the fog lifted and proceed. Later repairs cost $6,799.96.

3. May 4, 1931:

Departing Duluth, Minnesota, light for Ashland, Wisconsin, strong currents in the St. Louis River caused the vessel to rub hard on the corner of the Reiss Coal Dock #5 and this caused creases in plates abreast #2 cargo hold. Later repairs to the above waterline damage amounted to $6,003.00. The part about this departure that was highly unusual was that the REISS was enroute to Ashland to be loaded with anthracite coal which was on the Reiss Dock. It was overstock because of the lack of its need for fuel in the upper Midwest. When loaded, the ship departed for Milwaukee, Wisconsin where its cargo was unloaded and used locally.

4. November 14, 1934:

The vessel grounded off the south pier at Sheboygan, Wisconsin while inbound with 7,025 net tons of coal which had been loaded at Toledo, Ohio. Following lightering of the cargo, survey was made of the damage done during the grounding. Repairs were estimated to be in excess of $100,000. This was more than the ship was worth and a decision was made on December 8th to cut up the hull for scrap.

Steamer ROUMANIA

This oak-hulled bulk freighter was in the Reiss Fleet during 1916-1917. It had only one compartment in its hold and was not a versatile ship. It could usually only carry one type or grade of cargo because of this configuration. Its 2,600 gross ton carrying capacity also made it of restricted use. When commissioned in 1887, the ship boasted the first triple expansion engine ever installed on a Great Lakes vessel. Namesake of the carrier was the 91,700 square mile area in Eastern Europe of this name at the time of the vessel's christening.

A major stress of weather problem on June 24, 1916 while the ROUMANIA was upbound on Lake Superior caused the oak beams of the vessel to become twisted. It did not render the ship useless, but did restrict its future operation in foul weather.

Fleet Histories Series III

Steamer WILLIAM A. REISS (1) downbound in Little Rapids Cut, St. Mary's River, in 1927.

Steamer EDWARD U. DEMMER

Mr. Edward Uhrig Demmer was vice president and treasurer of the Milwaukee-Western Fuel Company of Milwaukee, Wisconsin in 1920 when this vessel took his name. That firm and The C. Reiss Coal Company had close ties and the Reiss Fleet carried major quantities of coal for the Milwaukee concern. The vessel was a typical bulk freighter of the day with four compartments in the cargo hold and a carrying capacity of 6,800 gross tons.

During operation in the Reiss Fleet in 1920 and 1921, this carrier had only one recorded mishap. That occurred at 1330 hours on July 6, 1920 with repairs to the damage running to $7,201.01. Strong current was running into the canal at Sault Ste. Marie, Michigan and caught the DEMMER's stern, causing her to sheer into the north pier. This happened even though the vessel was backing full speed to avoid striking. Ten frames were bent and two plates of whale strake were dented in the accident.

Steamer J. L. REISS

This vessel was delivered to its original owner on April 16, 1906. It was equipped with a triple expansion engine and two Scotch boilers, each of which carried 180 pounds of pressure per square inch. The engine had a shaft horsepower of 1,600. Mr. Jacob Ell Reiss was the namesake of this carrier. He was a member of the Reiss family but did not work in the coal business. Instead, he organized the International Tailoring Company in New York City and became its president in 1896. When this vessel took his name in 1920, he was back in Sheboygan and a director of several family businesses.

Steamer ROUMANIA upbound at the Soo Locks in 1917

Steamer EDWARD U. DEMMER upbound in Little Rapids Cut, St. Mary's River, during 1922.
There is no known photograph of the vessel in 1920 or 1921

As a bulk freighter in the Reiss Fleet, this vessel is known to have sustained six recorded accidents, as follows:

1. April 19, 1922, 2045 hours:

Drawing 16' forward and 18' aft, when entering the draw of the Louisiana Street Bridge at Buffalo, New York, the REISS rubbed heavily along the river bottom on its port bilge and bottom. At the time, it was in tow of the Tug TENNESSEE enroute to the Concrete-Central Elevator with a cargo of grain. Following unloading, the vessel was drydocked at Buffalo where repairs were made to the extent of $5,624.15.

2. September 10, 1924, 1625 hours:

The vessel was proceeding down the Niagara River to be unloaded of an iron ore cargo at North Tonawanda, New York and was drawing 18' 3" forward and 18' 6" aft. It grounded on the end of Rattlesnake Shoal which is largely a rocky bottom. Lightering of the ore was required to free the REISS and later repairs to her bottom at Buffalo amounted to $26,884.83.

3. July 11, 1925, 1100 hours:

While entering drydock at Manitowoc, Wisconsin, the ship rubbed the nearby railroad bridge and its rudder hit the dock which damaged both the rudder frame and some of the sideshell plating. Repairs were made which cost $3,026.82 for this accident.

4. December 4, 1926:

Upon docking at the Reiss Coal Dock in Sheboygan, and after being unloaded, cracked plates were discovered in the ship's double bottom. It was determined that the damage occurred from rubbing while entering the harbor. Leaking took place and the ship settled to the river bottom. It was pumped out of water, patched and towed to Manitowoc for repairs. Major plating and internals were found to be in need of renewal at a cost of $60,408.77.

5. July 21, 1927, 0935 hours:

Proceeding down the Niagara River with iron ore and heading between Red Nun and Black gas buoys, with the Motor Vessel MOTOR ISLAND over her stern, the REISS struck bottom when abreast of a small boat house and fish shanty on Grand Island. Substantial plate and internal damage was done in compartments #2, 3 and 4 on the starboard side and to #1 and 2 on the port side. After being unloaded, the carrier was drydocked at Buffalo where repairs were made to the sum of $20,043.81.

6. August 21, 1931:

The REISS had loaded a partial cargo of coal at the Irishtown Dock in Cleveland, Ohio and the dock superintendent called for a tug to assist the REISS in leaving the coal dock. The Tug VIRGINIA of the Great Lakes Towing Company was dispatched to perform this service. About 1300 hours, as the VIRGINIA arrived, another tug was called which was the T. C. LUTZ. The second call was made by the REISS because the vessel had been loaded "down by the head" and was drawing 14' forward but only 11' aft. When the LUTZ arrived, it was told it was not needed after all and it returned to the tug basin. At 1400 hours, the REISS departed the dock in tow of the VIRGINIA and proceeded down the Cuyahoga River.. After passing through the Baltimore & Ohio Railroad Bridge, the VIRGINIA dropped back on the port bow of the REISS, fastening the tow line on his cleat abreast the pilot house on the starboard side, assisting the REISS around the bend below the old Superior Viaduct. When the bow of the REISS was about abreast of the Upson-Walton Dock and the REISS was heading for the west draw of the Main Street Bridge, the VIRGINIA was lying idle on the bow of the REISS with her engine stopped. The REISS proceeded in this manner until her stem was about 100 feet above the center abutment of the Main Street Bridge. At about this time, the VIRGINIA backed without any signal from the REISS. This caused the REISS' stern to swing over to starboard, crushing a motor launch lying at the Upson-Walton Dock. The name of the launch was KILROY.

Captain Frankforther of the REISS stated that he blew three whistles for the tug to check, put his wheel hard to port and worked ahead to keep his stern away from the launch and dock, but was unable to do so and the launch was sunk lying at her moorings. The crew of the VIRGINIA denied being at power when the REISS blew and, therefore, could not have checked when the tug was not moving in the first place.

Later evidence showed that with the REISS loaded as she was, her wheel was so far out of the water that it could not hold the vessel steady and that if loaded more properly, she could have avoided the accident.

Following the launch sinking, the REISS proceeded lakeward with the assistance of the VIR-GINIA and was headed for the Lakefront Coal Dock in the Ellsworth Slip. The wind was blowing between 25 and 29 miles per hour and the VIRGINIA's captain informed the REISS that she would not assist the REISS into the slip if it was occupied by any other vessel when they arrived. When the REISS and its tug arrived at the slip, they observed the Steamer LOUIS W. HILL there loading coal. The tug asked to be relieved and stated that it would return to assist the REISS when the HILL departed. Following some mixed communication between the masters of the REISS and the VIRGINIA, the REISS did enter the Ellsworth Slip. When about one-third entered into the slip, the wind and current sagged the REISS down against Dock No. 23 of the Pennsylvania Railroad, striking the dock on the starboard side of the REISS. This caused the REISS to sheer to port, striking the HILL abreast her boiler house and causing some damage to the HILL, but considerably more damage to the port bow of the REISS. The REISS was judged to be entirely at fault in this accident and was ordered to pay all claims. These were for the sunken launch, the damage to Dock No. 23, the HILL and its own. All of this amounted to $89,770.55.

Steamer JOHN A. KLING

The self-unloading Steamer JOHN A. KLING was equipped with seven compartments in its cargo hold which could accommodate 9,000 net tons of coal or 10,400 gross tons of limestone or iron ore. It was also originally equipped with a triple expansion engine and two Scotch boilers. Its namesake was Mr. John Adam Kling who was president of Cleveland Builders Supply Company in 1922 when this vessel took his name.

During its time in the Rockport Steamship Company, the vessel was involved in ten recorded incidents, as noted below:

1. June 6, 1923, 1710 hours:
In making a landing for coal fuel at the Lime Island Dock, the vessel struck the dock and damaged three plates and two frames. Cost of repairs was $2,255.77.

2. September 2, 1923, 1806 hours:
While entering the area of Sturgeon Bay from the west, the Green Bay side, and making the turn to line up with Dunlap Reef Range, the vessel dragged on the bottom. At the time she was drawing 17' 3" forward and 17' 4" aft. Several plate fractures and indentations occurred, along with a number of rivets being torn away. Cost of repairs was $4,326.14.

3. September 28, 1924:
When departing Sandusky, Ohio with a cargo of coal, the ship stranded just outside the break-

Steamer J. L. REISS as a bulk freighter while upbound with coal at the Soo Locks in the spring of 1923.

wall due to a swift current. Bottom plating and bilges were seriously damaged. This resulted in drydocking and repair charges of $13,737.19.

4. April 27, 1925, 0134 hours:

The KLING was passing the Steamer EDWARD L. STRONG in the St. Clair River just below the Michigan Salt Works when the pair collided, doing damage to both ships. This occurred in the area of Marine City, Michigan. The KLING was found to be at fault and had to pay for the STRONG's repairs at a cost of $4,321.61 besides its own in the amount of $2,220.82.

5. July 14, 1925, 0935 hours:

In landing at Messner's Coal Dock at Houghton, Michigan, on the Keeweenaw Waterway, with a draft of 16' 3" forward and 17' 10" aft, the KLING rubbed on loose boulders just out of the channel. It began to take on water in #3 side tank as a result. A puncture was found with related holed plating and modest internal structural damage which cost $4,549.20 to repair.

6. May 4, 1926:

The KLING stranded at Rockport, Michigan on Lake Huron causing bottom plate damage (see below).

7. September 14, 1926:

Following striking of a coal dock in Toledo, Ohio and rupturing several side shell plates, the KLING was drydocked at Toledo. Upon inspection, total damage from the May 4th accident and this current one was found to amount to $14,770.05 in repair charges. A total of twenty-one plates required renewal.

8. July 31, 1928:

    The unloading boom cracked in half due to a belt breakdown and jamming of too much limestone being on the boom. Topside repairs were made in Cleveland, Ohio at a cost of $10,963.35 over a period of three weeks.

9. August 2, 1935:

    Following loading limestone at Kelley's Island, the KLING grounded upon attempting departure while drawing 18' 11" all around. Twelve bottom and six bilge plates were in need of renewal at a cost of $12,412.42.

10. November 12, 1935:

    The KLING struck a rock ledge above the 106th Street Bridge over the Calumet River in South Chicago, Illinois. It did damage to seven bottom plates and internals. Repairing these required drydocking in South Chicago with the total cost amounting to $6,083.20.

Steamer JOSEPH W. SIMPSON

    This composite-hulled bulk freighter was only in the Reiss Fleet for a short time and is not known to have sustained any mishaps. The vessel had a triple expansion engine and two Scotch boilers in its engine room. The namesake of the carrier was Mr. Joseph Warren Simpson who was president of the North Western Fuel Company of Milwaukee, Wisconsin when his name was chiseled on this bow in 1921. The company was a major receiver of lake-borne coal cargoes and a trans-shipper to various Midwestern destinations.

Steamer ALEX B. UHRIG

    The 4,900 gross ton carrying capacity bulk freight Steamer ALEX B. UHRIG was named for Mr. Alexander Bernhard Uhrig who was vice president of the Milwaukee-Western Fuel Company in 1919 when this carrier took his name. It was equipped with a triple expansion engine and two Scotch boilers.

    During its service in the Reiss Fleet, the UHRIG was known to have been involved in five accidents of consequence.

1. August 15, 1925, 0015 hours:

    While being towed down the river at Manitowoc, Wisconsin, stern first with the weather dark and foggy and the vessel dragging her port anchor, the ship struck some obstruction about 1,000 feet below the Manitowoc Cement Dock and 100 feet off the dock of the Manitowoc Shipbuilding Company. This happened despite the vessel's efforts to keep as near as possible in midchannel. The shoe, rudder and wheel were damaged with repairs amounting to $6,225.23.

2. May 13, 1926, 1830 hours:

    The steering gear parted at Southeast Bend, St. Clair River and the UHRIG sheered to port while upbound with coal. With the aid of her anchor and engine, she landed safely against the west bank of the river.. Later, full inspection showed damage was not so slight and that broken steering chains, quadrant, after winch and twenty-two bottom plates and internals were in need of repair. These cost $19,656.39.

3. April 27, 1927, 0500 hours:

    While proceeding up the Manitowoc River drawing 17' 10" forward and 18' aft, the UHRIG was in tow of the Tug ARCTIC when it sheered into the north bank of the river and grounded on rocky bottom. While on the strand, the water lowered somewhat, but afterwards rose sufficiently to release the vessel. Extent of the bottom and bilge damage amounted to $9,131.61 in repair cost.

4. June 26, 1935, 0715 hours:

Downbound, when ready to make a landing at the north pier at the Soo Locks, lock officials ordered the UHRIG to the Third Lock. Later, the same officials ordered her to the Fourth Lock at about the time the Third Lock was filling. The result of these maneuvers was that upon entering the Fourth Lock, the bow struck the middle pier on the starboard side just above the lock gates. The extent of damage to plating and framing was $7,381.50.

5. November 18, 1936, 1210 hours:

The UHRIG was proceeding upbound on Lake Michigan between North Manitou Light and Gray's Reef when a fish tug was spotted ahead raising its nets. The tug crossed directly into the side of the port bow of the UHRIG which split the tug in two from stem to stern. The pilot house floated freely away with five people clinging to it. The UHRIG's wheelsman on watch, Alvern M. Dishnow, and several others immediately launched a lifeboat which went to the men and rescued them, but with considerable difficulty. After review of this accident, the first mate of the UHRIG was suspended by the Coast Guard and the Reiss Fleet was held responsible for loss of the wooden tug. Total dollars involved in the restitution came to $22,896.77.

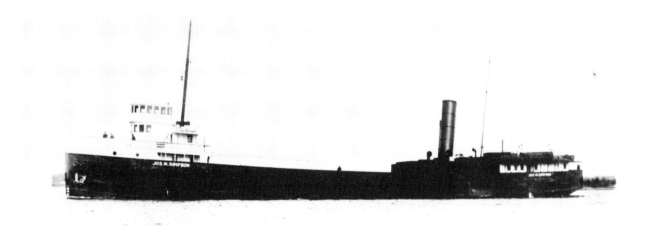

Steamer JOSEPH W. SIMPSON upbound in Little Rapids Cut, St. Mary's River, in 1924.

Steamer ALEX B. UHRIG passing downbound in the Detroit River as a bulk freighter.

Steamer ALEX B. UHRIG as a crane ship, downbound with pulpwood from L'Anse, Michigan in 1928.

Steamer JOHN A. KLING upbound at the Soo Locks during the 1925 navigation season.

Steamer WILLIAM K. FIELD

Namesake of this bulk freighter was Mr. William Kingsley Field. He was president of the Pittsburgh Coal Company in 1924 when this name was given to this carrier. During its entire career on the Great Lakes, the vessel was easily recognizable because of its three-tier pilot house which held extensive guest quarters and an observation deck.

While in the Reiss Fleet, the FIELD had two recorded incidents which are noted below:
1. November 26, 1926:

The ship stranded on the north end of Pipe Island Twin while upbound with a coal cargo destined for unloading at Duluth, Minnesota. The bow was out three feet forward and the forepeak was leaking. The Lighter T. F. NEWMAN came from Detour, Michigan to perform lightering of the cargo and the FIELD was released on November 29th. After proceeding to Duluth and being unloaded, the FIELD was drydocked at Superior, Wisconsin for repairs to her bottom plates. Cost of this work was $23,321.60.

2. May 6, 1928, 1720 hours:

The FIELD was downbound and attempting a landing at the north pier above the Soo Locks, and was backing instead of going to port because of windy conditions. The backing to starboard caused the port bow to strike the pier which resulted in damaging several plates. Later repair cost amounted to $5,737.03.

Steamer WILLIAM K. FIELD downbound in Little Rapids Cut, St. Mary's River, in the 1930 navigation season.

Steamer CHARLES C. WEST

Certain details of this vessel's unique construction were discussed earlier in this chapter. Mr. Charles Cameron West was its namesake. He was president of Manitowoc Shipbuilding Company in 1925 when the carrier was built. Two incidents are noted, as follows:

1. October 19, 1927, 1120 hours:
The WEST was navigating up the Buffalo River in Buffalo, New York with a cargo of limestone when, passing through the Ohio Street Bridge, it veered slightly to port and struck the Motor Vessel I. L. I.

103 while it laid at the Electric Elevator loading grain. Damage to the WEST was only superficial, but that of the motor vessel was considerable to her frames and plating on the starboard side. The damages paid by the WEST were $18,125.36.

2. September 7, 1929, 1100 hours:
    In passing through Gull Rock Passage in clear weather, the ship struck bottom on Gull Rock Reef. Thirty-six plates were damaged, along with many frames, rivets, etc. Drydocking and repairs came to $46,411.12.

Steamer LYNFORD E. GEER passing downbound in Little Rapids Cut, St. Mary's River, in 1926.

Steamer LYNFORD E. GEER

This vessel was delivered to its original owner on June 6, 1906. It was equipped with a triple expansion engine and two Scotch boilers. The boilers carried pressure of 170 pounds per square inch and the engine developed 1,500 shaft horsepower when operating at eighty-six revolutions per minute.

Namesake of the carrier was Mr. Lynford Elmer Geer. He was an original incorporator of the Manitowoc Shipbuilding Company and owner of ten shares of common stock on formation in 1902. He was serving as secretary-treasurer of the firm in 1926 when this vessel took his name. Two incidents are noted when this ship was in the Reiss Fleet under this name, as follows:

1. October 14, 1926, 1730 hours:
    In going through the lower Soo Line Railroad Bridge at Manitowoc, Wisconsin, the carrier fetched up on the river bottom. This caused twenty bottom and bilge plates to be damaged, along with frames bent and rivets lost. Repairs cost $14,572.23 at the local shipyard.

2. September 8, 1927, 1720 hours:
    Drawing 19' 2" forward and 19' 9" aft, the GEER was entering the Turnpike Bridge over the Buffalo Creek at Buffalo, New York and rubbed bottom. A grain cargo was aboard when the accident occurred. Relatively minor damage was done to plating and frames to the extent of $4,388.80.

Steamer CHARLES C. WEST upbound in the St. Mary's River on October 21, 1962

Steamer J. L. REISS

As a self-unloader, this vessel is known to have sustained four accidents while serving in the Reiss Fleet. They are:

1. August 13, 1934, 0705 hours:
The REISS was coming out of the Black Rock Channel and leaving the port of Buffalo, New York when the passenger Steamer CITY OF BUFFALO was coming into port. A slight collision between the sterns of the vessels occurred and the REISS was forced over and touched the bottom coming around on Waverly Shoal. Later repairs amounted to $29,755.22 to the REISS. The CITY OF BUFFALO paid its own damages.

2. August 7, 1935, 2340 hours:
Light and drawing 6' 6" forward and 15' 6" aft, while swinging into the Lakefront Coal Dock Slip at Cleveland, Ohio, the REISS struck the dock with her stem. She was being assisted by a tug at the time. Damage was done to the stem and plating on both port and starboard bows. Repairs were carried out at Lorain, Ohio between August 8th and 10th which cost $6,871.62.

3. July 29, 1940, 2250 hours:
The REISS had arrived at the Chesapeake & Ohio Coal Docks in Toledo, Ohio and commenced loading at 1900 hours. She finished taking on cargo and started to leave at this time, having blown a short

whistle to let go lines, then a long whistle as required under Rule No. 7 of the Pilot Rules for the Great Lakes. The REISS personnel then noticed the Steamer CLETUS SCHNEIDER backing around the end of the dock. The captain of the REISS observed that the SCHNEIDER was winding itself only with help from its mooring cables and he determined in his mind that there would be a collision between the two. He then blew a danger signal and backed full speed astern. The REISS had practically stopped when the stern of the SCHNEIDER struck the port bow of the REISS seven or eight feet from the stem. Inspection showed slight damage to the REISS in the area of the windlass room.

Captain R. W. England, arbitrator of the case, found that the owners of the SCHNEIDER were at fault as their vessel was not under control at the time of the accident. Reimbursement for later repairs to framing and plates in the amount of $13,798.67 was awarded to the REISS.

4. September 24, 1962, 0545 hours:
The Steamer J. L. REISS was in collision in the St. Clair River below Roberts Landing and above Willow Point with the Steamer SEWELL AVERY. The REISS was upbound with coal from Toledo, Ohio to Two Rivers, Wisconsin and had a draft of 16' 9" forward and 19' 6" aft. This particular morning, the REISS was following the upbound Steamer HENRY R. PLATT, JR. (2). The AVERY was loaded with limestone from Calcite, Michigan destined for Lorain, Ohio with a draft of 23' 8" forward and 24' 2" aft. Current in the area of the river involved generally is two to three miles per hour and downbound vessels run with the current.

As the AVERY proceeded downbound in the river, visibility became hazy and she decided to anchor. After the AVERY's engine was stopped and backed, her stern anchor was dropped at 0500 hours and she broadcast on the radiotelephone that she was anchoring.

In the meantime, the REISS was proceeding upbound at her regular speed of about eight miles per hour. The REISS encountered haze at about 0430 hours. She heard other vessels in the river and became aware of their movements. The REISS contacted another vessel further upstream and was advised that visibility was approximately 1/4 mile. The REISS was equipped with efficient radar and was using it. When the fog closed in at 0450 hours, the REISS' speed was checked to half speed, or about four miles per hour. Thereafter, the REISS maintained sufficient speed for steerageway. Upon encountering the fog, the REISS commenced sounding the prescribed three blast whistle signal for vessels underway in fog.

When the REISS heard the AVERY's radiotelephone message to the effect that she was going to anchor near Roberts Landing Buoy, the REISS observed on her radar the AVERY below Port Lambton near the Canadian shore. The AVERY was not near where she said she was going to anchor. By using the variable range finder on her radar, the REISS determined that the AVERY was then two miles below Roberts Landing Buoy (B-37) and that the AVERY was 1.2 miles upstream from the REISS, blending into the Canadian shoreline on the east shore of the river.

As the REISS encountered fog and commenced sounding her fog signals, the PLATT encountered the fog and was approximately two miles beyond the REISS. She also checked her speed and began sounding three whistle blasts. Since the PLATT was a more powerful and faster vessel than the REISS, the PLATT moved somewhat ahead of the REISS as the vessels approached Willow Point. Subsequent to checking her speed to half ahead upon encountering the fog, the REISS reduced her speed to slow ahead for short intervals with the result that her speed over the ground ultimately was two miles per hour when she passed Willow Point. Both the PLATT and the REISS constantly sounded their three blast fog signals at one minute intervals all the way up the stream. By thus sounding such signals, each was able to determine the relative position of the other as the two vessels continued upstream.

At 0516 hours, the REISS broadcast a security call on her radiotelephone advising that she was upbound in the vicinity of Willow Point. When she was near Buoy R-36, the REISS altered her course to port 358 degrees true on her gyro compass, the regular course for upbound vessels in the area of Willow Point and Roberts Landing. In view of the location of the AVERY close to the Canadian shore, the REISS made her turn further downstream than usual with the result that she was navigating close to the American shore. By this time the PLATT and she were within 4/10ths of a mile of one another. Both vessels held their bare steerageway and kept moving slowly upstream. Both the REISS and the PLATT heard the AVERY sounding the prescribed whistle signals at regular intervals. This signal was one short, two long and one short blast for a vessel at anchor in fog.

As the REISS passed Willow Point close to the American shore, the position of the AVERY had not changed. The REISS continued to sound three blast fog signals every minute as did the PLATT and the AVERY continued to sound anchor signals.

The REISS continued upstream close to the American shore and her captain constantly watched the target of the AVERY on his radar. There was no significant change in the target until the REISS was approximately 1,000 feet from the AVERY. It then was noted that the AVERY was moving out to the center of the channel and was crossways in the channel heading toward the American shore. When this situation became apparent to the REISS, the REISS' captain was surprised by this sudden change in the AVERY's position and he instructed the mate to call the AVERY and advise that she was drifting down on the REISS. The mate dialed in on Channel 51, the open channel constantly monitored on all vessels, and gave the message, but received no answer.

About the same time the call was completed, the AVERY was observed visually emerging out of the fog about 300 feet away. The REISS' rudder was put hard left and her engine was given full speed to try to avoid contact. The AVERY was first observed at a 90 degree angle to the REISS and moving rapidly ahead across the river in a westerly direction and swinging to her left, or downstream. The REISS called by voice to the AVERY that she was moving down on the REISS.

When the REISS' rudder was put hard left with her engine full speed ahead, she swung approximately 25 degrees to left after which her rudder was put hard right, her engine reversed to full astern and she dropped her starboard anchor. With the rudder hard right and her engine backing full astern, the REISS' heading swung back approximately 5 degrees to the right. The AVERY continued ahead with her bow swinging downstream until her stem, towing shackle and starboard bow struck the REISS' starboard side with a severe blow approximately 48 feet aft of the REISS' stem. The angle between the two vessels at the time of initial impact was about 35 degrees. After initial impact, the AVERY bounced away from the REISS and then struck her again on two subsequent occasions along the REISS' starboard side with resultant damage to the REISS in all there instances. At the time of the collision, the REISS had headway of approximately two miles per hour and the AVERY's speed was 5-6 miles per hour.

At the initial impact, the REISS was as close to the American shore as she could get with safety and she could not have moved over any more to her left, or to the west. The force of the collision caused the REISS to heel over to port and she was driven into the west submerged channel bank. Her port side aft struck the bank, causing damage to the REISS' port side.

After the AVERY dropped her stern anchor at 0500 hours, with almost the entire 70 fathoms, or 420 feet of chain out, she lost her headway and was stopped in the water. Although the AVERY's radar was in operation and reportedly working properly, her position in the river was not determined on radar. Consequently, in spite of the fact that her captain and first mate estimated that position, the AVERY's officers did not determine where the vessel was. Her anchor lights were illuminated and she commenced sounding the prescribed anchor whistle signals and bell signals. Visibility was then 200-300 feet and did not improve up to the time of the collision.

The AVERY's second mate, who was handling the controls on the stern anchor windlass, was then ordered by the captain to take in on the stern anchor chain. Thereafter, the AVERY's forward starboard anchor was dropped and subsequently the second mate reported that a pin had sheered on the stern anchor windlass. The first mate then was sent aft to help the second mate, leaving the captain as the only officer in the pilot house.

After the AVERY was motionless in the water on both anchors, it was noted on her gyro compass that her heading was slowly changing to right as a result of her stern drifting to port. It was apparent that current in the river was stronger than usual and this caused the stern anchor to drag with the consequent swing of the AVERY's stern. The AVERY's captain then called aft on the ship's telephone and learned that the stern was getting close to the Canadian shore. It was reported from the stern that lights and a boathouse were visible on the Canadian shore and there was concern about hitting the bank with possible damage to the AVERY's rudder shoe. The AVERY at this point got into the position seen on the radar of the REISS with her stern 450 feet from the Canadian shore and her bow extending out into the river.

The AVERY's starboard anchor was then raised and her engine was worked, first slow ahead for one minute, then half ahead for five minutes, then full speed ahead for nine minutes with her rudder hard left. The intended purpose was to swing the vessel's stern back toward the American side of the river. However, due to the current and her position crossways in the channel, the AVERY did not respond until after her engine had been worked full speed ahead. As a result of such action, the AVERY crossed from close to the Canadian shore toward the American shore traveling almost westerly across the river.

The AVERY's radar was located alongside the front window of her pilot house where the captain was stationed. It was turned on and was operating. However, the captain denied seeing either the REISS or the PLATT even though he claimed to have looked at the radar now and then. Moreover, crew members of the AVERY reported hearing whistle signals from the REISS and the PLATT as long as 35 minutes before the collision. For some time before the REISS was observed visually, the AVERY's third mate was reporting such whistle signals and pointing out to the captain the direction from which the signals were coming. Nevertheless, the captain denied hearing any fog signals or receiving any reports until just before the collision. The facts indicated, however, that the captain of the AVERY could hardly have failed to hear the signals, and thus knew of the approach of the REISS and the PLATT for at least one-half hour. It was found that he was so much concerned about the stern of his own vessel that he neglected the far more important duty of observation and safety of the REISS.

About a minute before the collision the AVERY's captain acknowledged the approach of the RE-ISS by the sound of her fog whistle close on the AVERY's port bow and then, looked at his radar. It was too late as the REISS was in such close proximity as to be out of the effective radar range. Only at this time did the AVERY sound a danger signal and back her engine. Thereafter, the REISS was observed visually about 100-150 feet away from the AVERY's port bow. The vessels came together rapidly in a very short period of time. After the collision, the AVERY was in a southwest and northeast position. In this position with 420 feet of anchor chain behind her, the AVERY actually was obstructing 1,050 feet of the width of the river and her forward end protruded into the flow of traffic.

When the REISS' port side aft hit the submerged channel bank, there was not much more than 52 feet between the AVERY's stem and the bank itself. This meant the only thing between the stem of the AVERY and the west bank was the REISS with its 52' width.

Both vessels came to rest in the river close to the American shore shortly after the collision, the REISS having dropped her starboard anchor and subsequently coming to rest on that anchor heading upstream. The AVERY came to rest heading downstream and dropped a forward anchor 10-20 minutes after the collision.

As one might expect in a collision case such as this, the matter was taken to court for final ruling of fault. The Court noted that the use of radar scopes by the REISS and the PLATT constantly informed them of their respective positions. Use by the AVERY of her radar would have informed the AVERY not only of her own position, but of the position of the REISS. The Court ruled that the AVERY's failure to notify the REISS of danger sooner constituted fault and negligence on the part of the AVERY. It also ruled that the REISS was not negligent in the matter and was without fault and that the collision would not have happened with proper lookouts and use of the radar on the AVERY in such dense fog conditions.

This 1965 ruling was appealed by the AVERY's owner. The Court of Appeals for the Sixth Circuit reversed the decision on March 16, 1967 and found both vessels to have been at fault.

Steamer J. L. REISS downbound in Lake St. Clair, as a self-unloader in 1940.

Steamer REISS BROTHERS

This handsome bulk freighter honored all eight sons of Clemens A. Reiss, the company's founder. From eldest to youngest these men were: Peter, Edmund, Jacob, John, Richard, William, Clemens, Jr. and Otto.

When serving in the Reiss Fleet under this name, this carrier is known to have sustained only one accident of significance. On July 28, 1952, while lying afloat at the Reiss Coal Dock in Superior, Wisconsin, and being unloaded of its coal cargo, the steamer was struck at 1140 hours by the Steamer BALL BROTH-ERS, doing damage to her port quarter, bulwarks, frames, angle bars and bulkhead. The Tug ILLINOIS was assisting the BALL BROTHERS into her unloading berth at the time.

Damage resulting in costs of $14,566.08 was tallied and paid for by the BALL BROTHERS to repair, afloat, seven shell plates, two bulwark plates, internal frames, port lights, a grocery davit, scuppers and the beading bar of the REISS BROTHERS.

Steamer OTTO M. REISS (2)

Namesake reference to this ship name was the same as for the first carrier in the Reiss Fleet to bear the name, as discussed earlier. No major incidents involved this vessel while in the Reiss Fleet under this name.

Steamer WILLIAM A. REISS (2)

As in the case of the previous vessel, the namesake reference for this bulk freighter was the same as for the first ship to bear the name in the Reiss Fleet. No accidents of note are recorded regarding the vessel while in the Reiss Steamship Company.

Steamer JOE S. MORROW

Mr. Joseph Sellwood Morrow was this bulk freighter's namesake. He was the grandson of Captain Joseph Sellwood and was born in 1890. Unfortunately, he died in 1911 before getting started in a career. His namesake was delivered to its original owner on April 15, 1907. It was equipped with a triple expansion engine and two Scotch boilers, each carrying 170 pounds per square inch of pressure.

Very early in its career in the Reiss Fleet, the vessel sustained an accident in what otherwise was an almost incident-free service. On April 14, 1937, while upbound with coal from Toledo, Ohio, the carrier was beached on Peach Island at the head of the Detroit River by Captain John Huff when it was reported to him that the vessel had sprung a leak and that the lower tanks were filling quickly. The captain determined that the only course of action for him to take, short of allowing the vessel to sink, was to beach her. This was done and relief vessels were called in. The Lighter RELIANCE was on the scene on the 15th along with a tug. Salvage operations commenced, but it was not until the 19th that 90% of the cargo was lightered and the MORROW was freed. She was patched for temporary repairs and pumps were put aboard to assist in keep-ing water pumped out as the carrier proceeded to Lorain, Ohio under its own power. There, it entered drydock for survey and repairs. On the 20th, there was found damage to fifty-four bottom plates, framing and internals. Two weeks of repair time was utilized at a cost of $27,767.88.

Steamer RICHARD J. REISS (2)

The namesake reference for this bulk freighter is the same as a vessel in the Reiss Fleet formerly bearing the same name. This carrier, however, was the newest and largest vessel in the fleet when commis-sioned in 1943. It was similar to the other fifteen Great Lakes bulk freighters built under a program of the U. S. Maritime Administration during World War II.

The REISS was involved in one noted accident during its service in this fleet as a bulk freighter. That occurred on November 4, 1945 and involved the Steamer LYMAN C. SMITH at Dock #3, Great

Northern Railway Ore Docks at Superior (Allouez), Wisconsin. A summary of the accident and finding of the Arbitrator in the case was issued at Detroit, Michigan by Mr. Carl V. Essery on August 5, 1948.

The SMITH had been loading iron ore at the east side of Dock #3. When four cars short of her full load, it became necessary to move to the west side of Dock #2 in order to complete her cargo. She was moored about halfway down Dock #3, starboard side to, bow headed in, and her stern about 1,000 feet shoreward from the outer end of the 1,956' ore dock. She blew one long blast of her whistle and, using her winches, with one line forward and one aft, hove along the dock until her stern was approximately at the outer end of the dock.

While the SMITH was engaging in heaving along the dock, the REISS, in water ballast and drawing 9' forward and 19' aft, arrived off Superior Harbor and began her passage through the Superior Entry at slow speed.

The master of the REISS first observed the SMITH when his vessel was in the vicinity of the breakwater light, 5,000 feet from the slip. The SMITH was in the position described earlier before she began to shift aft. It was the middle of the day with no inclement weather around. The main point of contention in the stories of the REISS and the SMITH was that the REISS claimed to have exchanged whistle signals with the ore dock, that she was proceeding under orders of the dock to the west side of #4 Dock to begin loading and that the SMITH knew of this exchange when she began to shift. The REISS construed the short blast of the SMITH to mean that she was casting off lines and the REISS replied with a danger signal, but this was not answered by the SMITH. After the SMITH had shifted, her position was such that she was partially blocking the entrance to the slip. Meanwhile, the REISS was proceeding towards her appointed berth on the west of Dock #4 at dead slow speed. The two vessels then exchanged passing signals at which time the REISS was about 800 feet astern and slightly off the port quarter of the SMITH. Soon, the stem of the REISS was lapping the stern of the SMITH about the time the SMITH put her engine half speed ahead, righted her rudder and began her first advance toward Dock #2. From this point on, with the REISS continuing to advance on a heading somewhere between 205 and 225 degrees and the SMITH continuing to work westward, one thing only could have occurred and that was for the sterns to come closer and closer to the point of collision.

The Arbitrator found that the REISS violated Rule 26 of the Great Lakes Rules of the Road because she did not give way to the SMITH under the circumstances of close navigation when the REISS was more maneuverable in her light condition. He also found the SMITH at fault for violating signal blasts which should have been followed, thus avoiding the collision. He stated, "The failure of the SMITH to discover the presence of the REISS in a timely season, her failure to appraise properly the dangerous situation which existed at the time she accepted the passing proposal, and her movements after accepting the two-blast signal, can be attributed only to faulty lookout or to resistance on her part to the demands implied in the signals from the REISS. Whichever may have been the reason for her failures, the SMITH cannot, in view of the provisions of Rules 27 and 28, be exonerated from fault contributing to the collision." The final ruling of the Arbitrator called for the REISS and the SMITH to each share equally in the total cost of repairs in the amount of $48,893.53.

Steamer SUPERIOR (3)

This vessel's basic data were written earlier when it was named RICHARD J. REISS (1). When the new carrier just described was commissioned, it was given this name which honored Lake Superior.

Steamer A. M. BYERS

The BYERS is shown here as she appeared following conversion to a self-unloader. While serving in the Reiss Fleet under this hull configuration, the BYERS suffered two notable accidents. The first resulted in her being sunk. The accident occurred at 2200 hours approximately 600 feet above Light No. 37 in the St. Clair River on April 19, 1956. It would prove to be the most serious accident on the Great Lakes that season.

The BYERS was loaded with a cargo of limestone from Drummond Island, Michigan and was passing downbound, destined for Buffalo, New York. The cement-carrying Steamer E. M. FORD was upbound and headed for its home port of Alpena, Michigan to load cement. As the vessels approached one another, the steering gear of the FORD failed. In spite of every effort to avoid it, a near head-on collision of the two ships resulted. Gapping holes were torn in the bows of both vessels by the impact. Since the FORD was in ballast, it was able to remain afloat though the collision forced her into shallow water near the shore. The BYERS, on the other hand, began to take on water heavily and sank on an even keel in 27' of water, leaving only her upper works and boom exposed above the water. The crew of the BYERS was taken ashore at Sans Souci where emergency relief was provided. The Coast Guard surveyed the BYERS and FORD quickly with a view to keeping the BYERS stabilized right side up until salvage workers and equipment could be brought alongside. Only one minor crew member casualty resulted from a bump on the head from a swinging door. The Coast Guard took over regulation of traffic past the BYERS during salvage operations as she was partially blocking the channel for downbound traffic. This persisted until temporary repairs were effected and the BYERS was pumped out and freed on May 8th.

The BYERS was towed to the shipyard at Toledo, Ohio for final survey and drydocking on May 9th and repairs were commenced. These were completed on July 2nd at a cost of $110,088.77.

The second accident of note for the BYERS as a self-unloader occurred on August 9, 1956 - a little over a month following repair of the damage sustained on April 19th! The BYERS was upbound in the St. Clair River with a coal cargo loaded at Sandusky, Ohio and destined for Hubbell, Michigan. The Steamer CUYLER ADAMS was downbound with grain from Duluth, Minnesota and destined for Buffalo, New York when she sheered into the BYERS while making a turn near Marine City, Michigan. Fault in the collision was determined to be that of the ADAMS and she was required to pay for the BYERS' repair costs in the amount of $35,416.24. The ADAMS' repairs amounted to $38,705.20. All of the damage was above the waterline and included cabins, bulwarks and internal frames on both vessels.

Steamer CLEMENS A. REISS (2)

The namesake reference for this vessel is the same as for the CLEMENS A. REISS (1). After taking this name in the Reiss Fleet, the vessel is not known to have sustained serious injury.

Steamer SUPERIOR (4)

Like the other vessel in the Reiss Fleet with this name, this carrier honored Lake Superior as its namesake. During its brief tenure in the fleet under this name, no known incidents occurred.

Steamer RAYMOND H. REISS

This was the last vessel to be acquired in the Reiss Fleet before it sale in 1969. Mr. Raymond Henry Reiss was the carrier's namesake. He was a board member of the fleet's parent coal company and president of Ronthor-Reiss Corporation of New York City.

The REISS was of Isherwood type construction which utilized longitudinal framing rather than the usual arch construction for strength in its hull. This method allowed the carrier greater carrying capacity at a given draft than a vessel of identical dimensions, and gave the vessel more limberness, especially in heavy seas. It was delivered to its original owner on August 26, 1916 by the building yard and originally was equipped with a vertical triple expansion engine and three Scotch boilers. It is not known to have sustained any accidents while in the Reiss Fleet.

Steamer REISS BROTHERS upbound in the St. Mary's River in 1963.

Steamer OTTO M. REISS (2) at the Reiss Coal Dock in Manitowoc, Wisconsin in 1961.

Steamer WILLIAM A. REISS (2) passing downbound in Little Rapids Cut, St. Mary's River, during the 1955 navigation season.

Steamer JOE S. MORROW passing upbound in the Detroit River in 1951

Steamer RICHARD J. REISS (2) as a bulk freighter, upbound in the Detroit River during the navigation season of 1957.

Steamer SUPERIOR (3) being towed for scrapping off the piers at Burlington, Ontario on May 2, 1947.

Steamer PETER REISS taking on a coal cargo at Cleveland, Ohio in 1966.

42

Steamer A. M. BYERS in her configuration as a self-unloader in 1955.

Steamer A. M. BYERS in her sunken condition following collision with the Steamer E. M. FORD on April 19, 1956.

Steamer CLEMENS A. REISS (2) being loaded with a cargo of coal at Cleveland, Ohio in 1967.

Steamer SUPERIOR (4) being unloaded at the Reiss Coal Dock in Superior, Wisconsin in 1959.

Steamer RICHARD J. REISS (2) passing upbound in the St. Mary's River on August 21, 1964.

Motor Vessel RAYMOND H. REISS passing upbound in Little Rapids Cut, St.Mary's River, in 1967.

STATISTICAL AND OTHER PERTINENT INFORMATION FOR VESSELS OF THE REISS AND AFFILIATED STEAMSHIP COMPANIES

Steamer WILLIAM RUDOLPH

Built: William Dulac Shipyard, Mount Clemens, Michigan - 1880
Hull No.: None assigned
Overall Dimensions: 152' x 23'6" x 9'
Years in Reiss Fleet: 1890-1905
Official Number: U. S. 80762
Other: Sold for scrap in 1914.

Schooner R. P. MASON

Built: T. W. Kirby Shipyard, Grand Haven, Michigan - 1867
Hull No.: None assigned
Overall Dimensions: 122' x 25' x 8'
Years in Reiss Fleet: 1890-1905
Official Number: U. S. 21877
Other: Swamped and sunk in a storm on Lake Michigan on June 20, 1917.

Steamer JOHN OADES

Built: W. H. Oades Shipyard, Detroit, Michigan - 1890
Hull No.: None assigned
Overall Dimensions: 220' x 36' x 24'
Years in Reiss Fleet: 1895-1904
Official Number: U. S. 76870
Other: Launched as a powered bulk freighter. Converted to a crane-equipped bulk freight barge in 1926. Abandoned in 1930.

Steamer BRAZIL
>Built: Union Dry Dock Company, Buffalo, New York - 1890
>Hull No.: 51
>Overall Dimensions: 290' x 40'2" x 24'4"
>Years in Reiss Fleet: 1905-1916
>Official Number: U. S. 3467
>Other: Launched as BRAZIL. Renamed GLENBRAE in 1919. Renamed BRAZIL, for the second time, in 1926. Converted to a sandsucker in 1929. Scrapped in 1948.

Steamer AMERICA (2)
>Built: Union Dry Dock Company, Buffalo, New York - 1889
>Hull No.: 48
>Overall Dimensions: 293' x 40'2" x 24'6"
>Years in Reiss Fleet: 1905-1916
>Official Number: U. S. 106638
>Other: Renamed GLENSTRIVEN in 1919. Stranded and abandoned in 1923. Sold for scrap in 1924.

Steamer BULGARIA
>Built: James Davidson Shipyard, West Bay City, Michigan - 1887
>Hull No.: 16
>Overall Dimensions: 306' x 40' x 22'
>Years in Reiss Fleet: 1908 and 1909
>Official Number: U. S. 3381
>Other: Scrapped in 1915.

Steamer A. M. BYERS/CLEMENS A. REISS (2)
>Built: American Ship Building Company, Cleveland, Ohio - 1910
>Hull No.: 448
>Overall Dimensions: 524' x 54' x 30'
>Years in Reiss Fleet: 1910-1954 (as bulk freighter), 1955-1958 (as self-unloader), 1959-1969 as CLEMENS A. REISS (2).
>Official Number: U. S. 207504
>Other: Launched as a bulk freighter. Converted to a self-unloader in 1955. Renamed CLEMENS A. REISS (2) in 1959. Renamed JACK WIRT in 1970. Sold for scrap in 1973.

Steamer JOHN P. REISS
>Built: American Ship Building Company, Lorain, Ohio - 1910
>Hull No.: 377
>Overall Dimensions: 524' x 54' x 30'
>Years in Reiss Fleet: 1910-1969
>Official Number: U. S. 207251
>Other: Sold for scrap in 1972.

Steamer PETER REISS
>Built: Superior Shipbuilding Company, Superior, Wisconsin - 1910
>Hull No.: 522
>Overall Dimensions: 524' x 54'3" x 30'
>Years in Reiss Fleet: 1910-1948 (as bulk freighter), 1949-1969 (as self-unloader).
>Official Number: U. S. 207471
>Other: Launched as a bulk freighter. Converted to a self-unloader in 1949. Sold for scrap in 1972.

Steamer FRANK T. HEFFELFINGER/CLEMENS A. REISS (1)/SUPERIOR (4)

Built: Chicago Shipbuilding Company, Chicago, Illinois - 1901

Hull No.: 49

Overall Dimensions: 450'6" x 50'3" x 28'6"

Years in Reiss Fleet: 1916 as FRANK T. HEFFELFINGER. 1917-1958 as CLEMENS A. REISS (1), 1959-1961 as SUPERIOR (4).

Official Number: U. S. 121205

Other: Sold for scrap in 1961.

Steamer OTTO M. REISS (1)

Built: Chicago Shipbuilding Company, Chicago, Illinois - 1901

Hull No.: 50

Overall Dimensions: 450' x 50' x 28'8"

Years in Reiss Fleet: 1916-1934

Official Number: U. S. 121208

Other: Launched as FREDERICK B. WELLS. Renamed OTTO M. REISS (1) in 1916. Renamed SULLIVAN BROTHERS (1) in 1934. Renamed HENRY R. PLATT, JR. (1) in 1957. Sold for grain storage, then scrap in 1966.

Steamer GEORGE W. PEAVEY/RICHARD J. REISS (1)/SUPERIOR (3)

Built: American Ship Building Company, Cleveland, Ohio - 1901

Hull No.: 310

Overall Dimensions: 450' x 50' x 28'

Years in Reiss Fleet: 1916 as GEORGE W. PEAVEY, 1917-1942 as RICHARD J. REISS (1), 1943-1947 as SUPERIOR (3).

Official Number: U. S. 86582

Other: Launched as GEORGE W. PEAVEY. Renamed RICHARD J. REISS (1) in 1917. Renamed SUPERIOR (3) in 1943. Sold for scrap in 1947.

Steamer WILLIAM A. REISS (1)

Built: American Ship Building Company, Lorain, Ohio - 1901

Hull No.: 309

Overall Dimensions: 450' x 50' x 28'6"

Years in Reiss Fleet: 1916-1934

Official Number: U. S. 121187

Other: Launched as FRANK H. PEAVEY. Renamed WILLIAM A. REISS (1) in 1916. Sold for scrap in 1935.

Steamer ROUMANIA

Built: James Davidson Shipyard, West Bay City, Michigan - 1887

Hull No.: 15

Overall Dimensions: 290' x 39' x 23'6"

Years in Reiss Fleet: 1916 and 1917

Official Number: U. S. 110733

Other: Abandoned in 1929 for age and hull condition.

Steamer EDWARD U. DEMMER

    Built: Detroit Shipbuilding Company, Wyandotte, Michigan - 1899

    Hull No.: 133

    Overall Dimensions: 440' x 50' x 28'

    Years in Reiss Fleet: 1920 and 1921

    Official Number: U. S. 107523

    Other: Launched as ADMIRAL. Renamed J. K. DIMMICK in 1913. Renamed EDWARD U. DEMMER in 1920. Sunk in 1923.

Steamer J. L. REISS

    Built: Detroit Shipbuilding Company, Wyandotte, Michigan - 1906

    Hull No.: 161

    Overall Dimensions: 500' x 52'3" x 30'

    Years in Reiss Fleet: 1920-1969

    Official Number: U. S. 202875

    Other: Launched as the bulk freighter W. K. BIXBY. Renamed J. L. REISS in 1920. Converted to a self-unloader in 1933. Renamed SIDNEY E. SMITH, JR. (2) in 1972. Sunk and demolished in 1972.

Steamer/Motor Vessel JOHN A. KLING

    Built: Manitowoc Shipbuilding Company, Manitowoc, Wisconsin - 1922

    Hull No.: 204

    Overall Dimensions: 561'3" x 56'3" x 30'3"

    Years in Reiss Fleet: 1922-1969

    Official Number: U. S. 222512

    Other: Launched as JOHN A. KLING. Renamed LEADALE (2) in 1981. Sold for scrap in 1983.

Steamer WILLIAM K. FIELD/REISS BROTHERS

    Built: Toledo Shipbuilding Company, Toledo, Ohio - 1924

    Hull No.: 176

    Overall Dimensions: 603' x 60'3" x 32'

    Years in Reiss Fleet: 1924-1969

    Official Number: U. S. 223607

    Other: Launched as WILLIAM K. FIELD. Renamed REISS BROTHERS in 1934. Renamed GEORGE D. GOBLE in 1970. Renamed ROBERT S. PIERSON in 1980. Renamed SPRUCEGLEN in 1982. Sold for scrap in 1985.

Steamer JOSEPH W. SIMPSON

    Built: Detroit Dry Dock Company, Wyandotte, Michigan - 1889

    Hull No.: 91

    Overall Dimensions: 256'9" x 42' x 23'3"

    Years in Reiss Fleet: 1923 and 1924

    Official Number: U. S. 92087

    Other: Launched as the bulk freighter MANCHESTER. Renamed JOSEPH W. SIMPSON in 1921. Renamed MINDEMOYA in 1938. Renamed YANKCANUCK (1) in 1946. Sold for scrap in 1959.

Steamer ALEX B. UHRIG
>Built: F. W. Wheeler & Company, West Bay City, Michigan - 1893
>Hull No.: 100
>Overall Dimensions: 378' x 45' x 27'
>Years in Reiss Fleet: 1923-1926 and 1931-1946 (as a bulk freighter). 1927-1930 (as a crane-equipped bulk freighter).
>Official Number: 126994
>Other: Launched as CENTURION. Renamed ALEX B. UHRIG in 1919. Sold for scrap in 1946.

Steamer LYNFORD E. GEER/OTTO M. REISS (2)
>Built: West Bay City Shipbuilding Company, West Bay City, Michigan - 1906
>Hull No.: 620
>Overall Dimensions: 440' x 52'3" x 28'
>Years in Reiss Fleet: 1926-1933 as LYNFORD E. GEER. 1934-1969 as OTTO M. REISS (2).
>Official Number: U. S. 203568
>Other: Launched as JAMES S. DUNHAM. Renamed LYNFORD E. GEER in 1926. Renamed OTTO M. REISS (2) in 1934. Sold for scrap in 1972.

Steamer CHARLES C. WEST
>Built Manitowoc Shipbuilding Company, Manitowoc, Wisconsin - 1925
>Hull No.: 216
>Overall Dimensions: 592' x 60' x 31'
>Years in Reiss Fleet: 1925-1969
>Official Number: U. S. 225066
>Other: Sold for scrap in 1978.

Steamer WILLIAM A. REISS (2)
>Built: Great Lakes Engineering Works, River Rouge, Michigan - 1925
>Hull No.: 251
>Overall Dimensions: 621'9" x 62' x 39'6"
>Years in Reiss Fleet: 1934-1969
>Official Number: U. S. 225045
>Other: Launched as JOHN A. TOPPING. Renamed WILLIAM A. REISS (2) in 1934. Sold for scrap in 1994.

Steamer JOE S. MORROW
>Built: American Ship Building Company, Lorain, Ohio - 1907
>Hull No.: 350
>Overall Dimensions: 440' x 52' x 28'
>Years in Reiss Fleet: 1937-1969
>Official Number: U. S. 203908
>Other: Sold for scrap in 1973.

Steamer RICHARD J. REISS (2)
>Built: Great Lakes Engineering Works, River Rouge, Michigan - 1943
>Hull No.: 290
>Overall Dimensions: 620'6" x 60'3" x 35'
>Years in Reiss Fleet: 1943-1963 (as a bulk freighter), 1964-1969 (as a self-unloader).
>Official Number: U. S. 243406
>Other: Launched as the bulk freighter ADIRONDACK. Renamed RICHARD J. REISS (2) in 1943. Converted to a self-unloader in 1964. Renamed RICHARD REISS in 1986. Still in service.

Motor Vessel RAYMOND H. REISS

Built: American Ship Building Company, Lorain, Ohio - 1916

Hull No.: 715

Overall Dimensions: 600' x 60' x 32'

Years in Reiss Fleet: 1965-1969

Official Number: U. S. 214318

Other: Launched as EMORY L. FORD. Renamed RAYMOND H. REISS in 1965. Sold for scrap in 1980.

THE PEAVEY STEAMSHIP COMPANY

The Peavey Steamship Company was identified with Great Lakes shipping during the early part of this century, but the Peavey name remained synonymous with grain merchandising and shipping well into the 1970's when the company was sold to Con-Agra, Incorporated. The Peavey Grain Company of Minneapolis, Minnesota decided to float its own grain in its own Great Lakes vessels instead of using trip-chartered carriers owned by others in 1900. Their shipments essentially were over a trade route from Duluth/ Superior to their grain elevator and mill at Buffalo, New York. This management decision led to the incorporation of the Peavey Steamship Company, with papers being filed in Charleston, West Virginia on December 26, 1900. The original incorporators, directors and officers were not Peavey personnel, but acted on their behalf. They were: Messrs. Benjamin P. Bole - treasurer, James H. Hoyt - vice president, Henry H. McKeehan - president, William C. Merrick - director and Gustav von den Steinen - secretary. These gentlemen paid-in one hundred dollars each to accommodate the minimum sum of $500.00 paid-in capital under West Virginia law, and each man held one share of the five original shares issued.

It was stated in the Articles of Incorporation that the company "desired the privilege of increasing the said capital, by sale of additional shares from time to time, to $400,000.00 in all." The stated purpose of the company was that "of doing a general transportation business." Articles also stated that the corporation "shall keep its principal office, or place of business, at Duluth, Minnesota."

At a planned special meeting of the board of directors in a branch office of the company, in the Western Reserve Building in Cleveland, Ohio, at 1730 hours on January 15, 1901, the following parties were present: Messrs. Frank H. Peavey, Francis T. Chamberlain, Frederick M. Prince, James C. Wallace, John W. Raymond, James H. Hoyt, William E. Fitzgerald and Augustus B. Wolvin. Mr. Wolvin acted in the capacity of Trustee for the proposed vessels that would be built. Ownership of shares in the steamship company of the above meeting attendees was as follows: F. H. Peavey - 2,050, F. T. Chamberlain - 20, F. M. Prince - 50, J. C. Wallace - 100, J. W. Raymond - 50, J. H. Hoyt - 50, W. E. Fitzgerald - 50. A total of 2,370 shares were represented. Frank H. Peavey was elected president and James H. Hoyt was elected secretary. At this meeting, the directors and shareholders ratified the actions of December 26, 1900 and accepted "the proposition made to the company by Augustus B. Wolvin, Trustee, dated January 15, 1901" to manage the new vessels for Peavey and to orchestrate their construction.

In another special meeting of the board on May 22, 1901, all of the original directors and officers resigned, though a few were re-elected to new posts. The new alignment of officers thereupon was: Messrs. Frank H. Peavey - president, George W. Peavey - vice president, Charles F. Deaver - treasurer, James H. Hoyt - secretary. Messrs. Wolvin and William L. Brown served as directors only while Frank and George Peavey were the other directors as well as officers.

Mr. Wolvin, as Trustee, entered contracts for four ships to be built in 1901. They were subject to $700,000.00 First Mortgage Bonds to be taken by the American Ship Building Company in part payment for the vessels. In consideration of the payment to Wolvin, as Trustee, of $500.00, and the issuance to him or his nominees, of 3,995 shares of the capital stock of the Peavey Steamship Company, and twenty-four notes of $3,333.33 each, all as stated in Wolvin's proposition to the company, construction work began. The notes were intended to pay for the boilers of the new carriers at $20,000.00 each. They were payable to Babcock & Wilcox Company "on or before three, six, nine, twelve, eighteen and twenty-four months from the date when the respective steamers went into commission."

It was resolved at the May 22nd meeting "that a branch office of the company be established at Minneapolis, Minnesota" and that "all meetings of directors and shareholders may be held there."

Part of Mr. Wolvin's proposition called for him to manage the vessels when they were commissioned and he did this from 1901 until mid-1913. His involvement in the confederation of lines to form Canada Steamship Lines in 1913 was the reason his services were terminated at that time. It was reasoned by Peavey personnel that there may be a conflict of Wolvin's interest in working with Peavey and a foreign steamship operation. Thus, the Duluthian's Peavey connection was severed, but another Duluth resident was chosen by Peavey to manage the fleet. This was Mr. George Ashley Tomlinson, himself a long-time vessel owner and operator. He continued to manage the Peavey Fleet until its sale to the Reiss Steamship Company of Minnesota.

At a special meeting of stockholders of the Peavey Steamship Company on March 20, 1916, in an office at 312 Chamber of Commerce Building in Minneapolis, Minnesota at 1000 hours, Messrs. Frederick B. Wells and C. F. Deaver represented the Peavey shareholders and acted as president and secretary, respectively. There appeared in person only these two gentlemen, plus Charles W. Lane with proxies in hand for the other 5,760 shares issued and outstanding. By unanimous consent, sale of the four Peavey bulk freighters was approved and they were sold to Reiss for $250,000 each, plus the assumption of the outstanding bonded indebtedness of $54,000.00 on each vessel. The net cash price to Peavey, therefore, was $196,000.00 per vessel. This sum was payable at the time of delivery of the steamers. The broker in this transaction was D. Sullivan & Company of Chicago, Illinois who was paid a total of $5,000.00 in commissions for its services in the negotiations. Official transfer of the four ships was made the same date on Government books in Wilmington, Delaware.

The four Peavey freighters carried black hulls with white cabins. Their stacks were also black with a red diamond centered on them. The letters "Pv," standing for the parent firm's logo, were centered in the diamond in white letters.

It should be noted that of the total shares issued and outstanding, 3,330 were held by the F. H. Peavey Company. A few of the other large shareholdings were in the names of the following: Messrs. J. H. Wade - 450, A. L. Searle - 390, John J. Mitchell -315 and G. H. Christian - 292.5 shares. Throughout its life, the major shareholder of Peavey Steamship was either Frank H. Peavey or his grain firm. When it seemed appropriate to get out of the shipping business, sell the vessels and arrange a long-term floating contract with the ships' buyer, there was little doubt that Frank Peavey could do as he pleased.

Over the next few years, the company continued to have a corporate charter, but it was in name only. Final dissolution of Peavey Steamship Company occurred when its charter was cancelled on September 29, 1919.

Steamer FRANK T. HEFFELFINGER

Mr. Frank Totten Heffelfinger was a son-in-law of Mr. Frank H. Peavey, the Peavey Company's founder. He was also a vice president of F. H. Peavey & Company in 1901 when this vessel took his name. He later became president of the company in 1906 and served in that post until 1945.

During this carrier's tenure in the Peavey Fleet, it is known to have sustained two accidents which are capsulized below:
1. August 11, 1913, 0245 hours:
The HEFFELFINGER was downbound with grain in the stretch of lower Lake Huron between the intersection of the Point Edward Light and Fort Gratiot Ranges and the Lake Huron Lightship No. 51. The Steamer JOHN ERICSSON was upbound and towing the Barge MAIDA at the time of the collision.

A short distance below the Lightship, the HEFFELFINGER passed the upbound Steamer R. W.

ENGLAND under one blast signals, and at about the same time, exchanged one blast signals to a following steamer whose lights indicated she had a tow. The HEFFELFINGER passed the ERICSSON safely at about seventy-five feet and then the barge was seen with her stern sagging down across the HEFFELFINGER's bow. The HEFFELFINGER blew a danger signal and the ERICSSON also blew a danger signal. The HEFFELFINGER's wheel was put hard aport and she started to swing, but in spite of all this the port quarter of the barge struck the HEFFELFINGER's port bow. Weather conditions were clear, but there was a strong wind from the east across the channel.

The ERICSSON was towing the MAIDA on a tow line about 550' in length. The wheelsman on the barge claimed that he kept his wheel within a turn of hard aport until just prior to the collision, while the mate of the barge said only a "little wheel" to port was being used. This whole matter was brought to arbitration before Mr. George L. Canfield of Detroit, Michigan for settlement.

Mr. Canfield found that the HEFFELFINGER did not sheer under the circumstances described by both parties. He also found that the HEFFELFINGER was at fault for not passing the ERICSSON with more than about 75' when the channel was wider to allow more clearance, especially when the master knew that the ERICSSON had a barge in tow. On the other hand, he ruled that the ERICSSON's master should have made more allowance for the swing of his barge in such close quarters as the channel dictated, given the wind conditions which might tend to blow an upbound, unpowered vessel into the path of a downbound vessel. In addition, the MAIDA had no light on its stern visible to the HEFFELFINGER so that the HEFFELFINGER could not see the position of the MAIDA's stern until just before the collision.

In summation of his decision, Mr. Canfield found that all three vessels used less than proper judgment in the matter and decreed that the $28,899.63 in total damages should be split equally between the owners of the HEFFELFINGER and the ERICSSON and MAIDA. In reality, this amounted to an award of one-third of the costs to the Peavey Steamship Company and two-thirds of the cost to the Pittsburgh Steamship Company, owners of the ERICSSON and MAIDA.

2. September 3, 1915, 0100 hours:

This accident involved the Erie & Western Transportation Company's Steamer ALLEGHENY and the HEFFELFINGER in the Detroit River. The ALLEGHENY was loaded with 2,400 net tons of package freight and was upbound in the Detroit River in the vicinity of River Rouge. She was following the upbound Steamer D. R. HANNA at the time, until the HANNA and ALLEGHENY were abreast Smith's Coal Dock. At this time, the ALLEGHENY passed the HANNA on the latter's starboard side. The weather was clear and lights of other vessels and the cities on both sides of the river were quite visible.

The ALLEGHENY was running at half-speed and, after passing the HANNA, discovered above her the masthead of the HEFFELFINGER about 1,500' away on the starboard side. No signal had been heard from the HEFFELFINGER, but just about that time the HANNA blew the HEFFELFINGER a signal of two blasts. No answer was heard. Immediately after this the range and red lights of the HEFFELFINGER became visible. At this time, the ALLEGHENY was headed practically straight up the river and the HEFFELFINGER was heading somewhat to westward, or the American shore. When the masthead light was seen on the ALLEGHENY's starboard bow, an order was given to starboard a little, but before the order was executed the red range lights of the HEFFELFINGER opened. The ALLEGHENY's wheel was then put hard aport and a one-blast signal was blown, which the HEFFELFINGER answered with one, and the ALLEGHENY's engine was immediately put to full speed ahead. Just as the throttle was opened the collision occurred at a point about three lengths from the Sandwich Coal Dock and about 300' east of mid-channel. The HEFFELFINGER's port bow struck the ALLEGHENY's port bow just forward of #1 hatch. Directly after answering the ALLEGHENY's one-blast signal, the HEFFELFINGER blew an alarm and, being on the swing to port heading between the ALLEGHENY and the HANNA's course but failing to stop her swing, collided with the ALLEGHENY. The ALLEGHENY's lights were burning at all times before and after the collision. After the first impact, the bow of the HEFFELFINGER went to starboard and her stern to port, while the ALLEGHENY did the same, and this brought the steamers together again aft. The port quarter of the HEFFELFINGER struck the ALLEGHENY's #6 gangway as a result of this maneuver.

On behalf of the HEFFELFINGER it was contended that she was bound down the Detroit River, and while moving along at slow speed not over three miles per hour in the vicinity of River Rouge, an upbound steamer, which proved to be the HANNA, blew a two-blast passing signal which was promptly answered by two blasts. The course of the steamer was so shaped that she would pass between the HANNA and a large steamer at anchor near the middle of the river. This proved to be the Steamer SHENANGO. With the same rate of speed, the HEFFELFINGER continued on her course when suddenly from under the stern of the SHENANGO the ALLEGHENY emerged, heading so that her course took her across the bow of the HEFFELFINGER. Nothing had been seen of the ALLEGHENY before this. The steamers were so close when this was evident, the HEFFELFINGER blew a danger signal and ordered full astern. The ALLEGHENY directed her course to starboard with the evident intention of passing port and port between the HEFFELFINGER and SHENANGO, but was unable to swing far enough and struck the HEFFELFINGER on her port bow with her own port bow. This was followed with a second collision while she was swinging clear.

As might be suspected, owners of the HEFFELFINGER and ALLEGHENY could not agree on fault. The matter was put before Mr. Charles E. Kremer, as Arbitrator, and he decided thusly, in part, at Chicago, Illinois on April 3, 1917:

"The atmosphere was clear and visibility was good to both sides of the river and to upbound and downbound traffic. The smoke of the SHENANGO was blowing in such a way as to mask the view of the HEFFELFINGER from the ALLEGHENY and vice versa. I am satisfied that the ALLEGHENY coming out from under the stern of the SHENANGO at nearly full speed into the immediate presence of the HEFFELFINGER was the immediate cause of the collision. In my judgment it was then too late to avoid a collision unless it might have been done had the ALLEGHENY starboarded instead of porting her helm. The situation was one "in extremis," and under such circumstances the courts hold the ship liable which creates the "in extremis" situation. In this case, the situation was due to the negligence of the master of the ALLEGHENY." The ALLEGHENY's faults were enumerated as follows:

1. She was passing the HANNA without obtaining permission.
2. Her master did not hear the answer of the HEFFELFINGER to the passing signal of the HANNA.
3. The master erroneously claimed the HANNA's signal was blown after the ALLEGHENY discovered the HEFFELFINGER.
4. His testimony that there was an exchange of one-blast of the whistles with the HEFFELFINGER is not borne out by the evidence.
5. The ALLEGHENY's claim to having been 1,500 feet away from the HEFFELFINGER when she observed her at first is not borne out; rather she was more like 500 feet away.
6. The ALLEGHENY was proceeding at too high a rate of speed under the circumstances.

"I, therefore, find and award that the owner of the ALLEGHENY must bear the damages sustained by her, and pay the damages sustained by the HEFFELFINGER."

It was later noted that total damages were $23,008 for the HEFFELFINGER and $12,677 for the ALLEGHENY.

Steamer FRANK H. PEAVEY

This steel bulk freighter's namesake was Mr. Frank Hutchinson Peavey. He was the founder of F. H. Peavey & Company and its president in 1901 when this carrier took his name. This 7,000 gross ton carrying capacity vessel was the first of the four sisterships built for the company to be commissioned in 1901.

During its service in the Peavey Fleet, the vessel is known to have sustained one recorded accident, and it was not of a major nature. It occurred on July 5, 1913 while the ship was being towed out of the River Bed Dock in the Cuyahoga River at Cleveland, Ohio. Two tugs were assisting, with one on the stern and one on the bow as the PEAVEY was proceeding stern first towards the main channel of the river. When at the fork of the main river, the PEAVEY was struck by the Steamer CITY OF THE STRAITS, receiving dented plates on the starboard side of her bow and damage to internal frames. Damage to the striking combination passenger and package freighter was minimal. Total cost of repairs amounted to $11,946.77.

Steamer GEORGE W. PEAVEY

This bulk freighter was delivered to the Peavey Steamship Company on October 20, 1901. It was equipped with a quadruple expansion engine and two Scotch boilers. The engine developed 1,700 shaft horsepower and the boilers carried a 250 pounds per square inch pressure rating. Normal speed of the vessel in a loaded condition was twelve miles per hour.

Mr. George Wright Peavey was this carrier's namesake. He was the son of Frank H. Peavey and active in the grain firm, but retired in 1906 when the company was incorporated. He then sold his interest in the company to his two cousins.

Steamer FREDERICK B. WELLS

Mr. Frederick Brown Wells was a son-in-law of Frank H. Peavey in 1901 when this steel bulk freighter took his name. When F. H. Peavey & Company was incorporated in 1906, he was elected vice president. Though it is not clear, it is reasoned that Mr. Wells took the job that was originally intended for George W. Peavey had he remained with the grain merchandising firm.

During its tenure in the Peavey Fleet, the carrier is not known to have been involved in any serious mishaps.

Steamer FRANK T. HEFFELFINGER upbound with coal above the Soo Locks in 1912.

Steamer FRANK H. PEAVEY passing upbound with coal above the Soo Locks in 1913.

Steamer GEORGE W. PEAVEY upbound in the St. Clair River in 1910.

Steamer FREDERICK B. WELLS passing downbound near the Soo Locks in 1913.

STATISTICAL AND OTHER PERTINENT INFORMATION FOR VESSELS OF THE PEAVEY STEAMSHIP COMPANY

Steamer FRANK T. HEFFELFINGER

> Built: Chicago Shipbuilding Company, Chicago, Illinois - 1901
> Hull No.: 49
> Overall Dimensions: 450'6" x 50'3" x 28'6"
> Years in Peavey Fleet: 1901-1916
> Official Number: U. S. 121205
> Other: Launched as FRANK T. HEFFELFINGER. Renamed CLEMENS A. REISS (1) in 1917. Renamed SUPERIOR (4) in 1959. Sold for scrap in 1961.

Steamer FRANK H. PEAVEY

> Built: American Ship Building Company, Lorain, Ohio - 1901
> Hull No.: 309
> Overall Dimensions: 450' x 50' x 28'6"
> Years in Peavey Fleet: 1901-1916
> Official Number: U. S. 121187
> Other: Launched as FRANK H. PEAVEY. Renamed WILLIAM A. REISS (1) in 1916. Sold for scrap in 1935.

Steamer GEORGE W. PEAVEY

> Built: American Ship Building Company, Cleveland, Ohio - 1901
> Hull No.: 310
> Overall Dimensions: 450' x 50' x 28'
> Years in Peavey Fleet: 1901-1916
> Official Number: U.S. 86582
> Other: Launched at GEORGE W. PEAVEY. Renamed RICHARD J. REISS (1) in 1917. Renamed SUPERIOR (3) in 1943. Sold for scrap in 1947.

Steamer FREDERICK B. WELLS

> Built: Chicago Shipbuilding Company, Chicago, Illinois - 1901
> Hull No.: 50
> Overall Dimensions: 450' x 50' x 28'8"
> Years in Peavey Fleet: 1901-1916
> Official Number: U. S. 121208
> Other: Launched as FREDERICK B. WELLS. Renamed OTTO M. REISS (1) in 1916. Renamed SULLIVAN BROTHERS (1) in 1934. Renamed HENRY R. PLATT, JR. (1) in 1957. Renamed PILLSBURY BARGE in 1959. Sold for scrap in 1966.

GARTLAND STEAMSHIP COMPANY
and its affiliated companies

This fleet's founder was Captain Denis Sullivan. He was born in Dublin, Ireland in 1849 and moved with his parents to Dunnville, Ontario in the 1850's. While receiving his education locally, he became aware of shipping on the Great Lakes. This was easy for the young man since Dunnville is located only a few miles upstream from Port Maitland, then a vibrant port-of-call for Lake Erie steamers. Dunnville was also accessible to shallower draft vessels.

Denis Sullivan began sailing the Great Lakes about 1866 and received his master's license in the early 1870's. He settled in the Milwaukee, Wisconsin area in 1873 and became acquainted with the numerous ship management and ownership firms then located in that city. As events turned out, Captain Sullivan impressed Mr. David Vance, a prominent Milwaukee shipowner and manager, with his credentials and Vance awarded him with command of the new Schooner MOONLIGHT which was built by the Wolf & Davidson Shipyard for Vance. The carrier was delivered in April, 1874. This impressive schooner was under Captain Sullivan's command from its first voyage through the navigation season of 1885.

The MOONLIGHT measured 213 feet in overall length, 33'6" in breadth and 14' in depth. The three-masted schooner had a mainmast that towered 105 feet into the air! It spread an enormous footage of canvas.

The MOONLIGHT had a carrying capacity of 1,400 net tons of cargo and a reputation of being "fast as a Clipper." In fact, newspapers of the day commonly referred to the MOONLIGHT as the "Queen of the Lakes." She would regularly make the run between Chicago, Illinois and Buffalo, New York, a distance of some 895 statute miles, in a little under four days. In a normal season, the vessel would make eleven round trips between lower Lake Michigan and eastern Lake Erie ports.

Captain Sullivan was unwed upon his arrival in Milwaukee. In due course, he met a lady who would become his wife whose name was Ella Gartland. She and her family were originally from Herkimer County, New York before establishing residence in Milwaukee. The couple was married in 1878 and it was her maiden name that became the namesake of the Gartland Steamship Company.

It was noted that Captain Sullivan sailed the MOONLIGHT through 1885. He then became the major investor in Hull 24 which was committed for construction by the Milwaukee Shipyard Company in 1886. The vessel was a wooden bulk freighter which was launched September 9, 1886. It measured 210 feet in overall length, 34'6" in breadth and 19' feet in depth. It was christened Steamer VERONICA in honor of the wife of Mr. Conrad Starke, owner of the Milwaukee Tug Company for whom the ship was built. Captain Sullivan took command of the VERONICA upon its completion and sailed her through the close of navigation in 1888. Thereupon, he joined the shore staff of David Vance & Company as marine superintendent in 1889.

Captain Sullivan became acquainted with Captain William Geddes Keith in 1891. He was a man of similar background who was involved in vessel ownership, management and marine insurance brokerage in Chicago, Illinois. The pair decided to create a partnership in the same line in 1892 and Captain Sullivan and his family moved to Chicago to activate this arrangement.

Captain Keith was the senior man, having been born in 1826 in Caithness-shire, Scotland. At the time of the partnership's formation, Captain Keith held ownership shares in several Great Lakes vessels, including the wooden Steamer CITY OF LONDON (3) which had been built the previous year to serve in the general bulk trades. It had an overall length in excess of 300 feet.

As the partnership prospered, Captain Sullivan also advanced in Great Lakes shipping circles. He was elected a member of Lake Carriers' Association and their Board of Managers in this time frame. He also established a valuable reputation in the marine insurance and brokerage business. At the turn of the century the partnership was dissolved, at least partly because of Captain Keith's advanced age and health. He died in 1902. As a result of this, Captain Sullivan operated the business as a sole proprietorship until bringing his son, Arthur, into the firm as a partner in 1904. This firm continued to perform the various functions previously carried on by the earlier partnership and set up offices in the Brother Jonathan Building which was close to the former building of the Chicago Board of Trade on Jackson Boulevard in downtown Chicago.

In the early days of commerce on the Great Lakes, vessels were owned "on shares." That is, when a vessel was built, a number of individuals each owned an interest in her, subscribing various amounts of capital as their interests appeared on the record. This, of course, applied mainly to entrepreneurs. Large companies built and owned their own vessels, but there were few large companies in the early days to do so. The names and the amounts of each ownership were then recorded on the vessel's documents. In legal terms, these interests were "joint and several." Each year the vessel operated the share owners put up funds to fit out the ship and get her started in the season. At the end of the year, they received their share of the voyage revenues. The share owners also assumed all the liabilities and the risk of all losses. These arrangements were on a "share and share alike" basis. The owners also hired a manager who obtained cargoes, hired the crew, looked after maintenance and repair and, in all respects, "husbanded" the ship.

An ownership interest alternate was "ownership in Trust." The Manchester Trust was one of these and it was managed by D. Sullivan & Company. It is of interest to note that the Manchester Trust was the namesake of the composite-hulled Steamer MANCHESTER when it was built in 1889. The vessel was first built, then its ownership was vested in the Manchester Trust. This had the effect of hiding the fact of the real ownership, which in this case was Ella Gartland Sullivan. This arrangement was not uncommon prior to 1900 when the corporate device came into general use for the ownership of vessels.

As well as acting in the capacity of vessel managers, D. Sullivan & Company personnel were port agents for vessels under the management of others. For this they received a commission or a fixed fee. For arranging cargo for ships under their own management as well as others, D. Sullivan also received brokerage, or a commission fee. As noted earlier, the Sullivan firm was also active in the role of insurance brokers. This activity began with the practice in the grain trade of insuring a valuable cargo against damage or loss. The vessel managers placed this insurance with underwriters of each cargo and collected a commission for doing so. From this point, it was only a short step to arranging hull and total loss insurance for the vessels under the firm's management.

D. Sullivan & Company was quite profitable from the start and it took its first major vessel management in 1902 when the firm agreed to manage three vessels for the West Division Steamship Company. That firm had been managed by Vance & Company of Milwaukee through 1901 with Mrs. William H. (Marion) Wolf serving as its president and treasurer. During this Vance management, West Division Steamship was not a corporation. The Articles to form the company as a Wisconsin corporation were filed April 22, 1901 with Marion Wolf and Lottie V. Dyer as the incorporators. Head offices were established at 236 Oneida Street in Milwaukee and the Vance management continued through 1901. Capitalization was established at $225,000.00. The principal officers of the firm as a corporation were: Marion A. Wolf - president, Lottie V. Dyer - vice president and Adda M. Becher - secretary. Other directors were Marion R. Pingree and James Mowatt. Most of the above-named ladies were widows of former marine executives in Great Lakes transportation. The West Division Steamship Company was dissolved by unanimous vote of the shareholders on February 26, 1914 with all 2,250 outstanding shares being voted.

The three vessels of the company had black hulls with white bow upper bands and the letters "W.D.S.S. Co." in white letters just below the band. The stacks were solid black.

Carriers in West Division Steamship were the Schooner-Barge ARMENIA (3) and the Steamers FRED PABST and WILLIAM H. WOLF (1). During management by D. Sullivan, the Schooner-Barge ARMENIA (3) was swamped and sunk in a severe storm near Colchester Reef, Lake Erie on May 9, 1906. The FRED PABST was in a collision on October 11, 1907 with the Steamer LAKE SHORE in the St. Clair River and passed out of the fleet, although the hull served as a lighter before its abandonment in 1920. The WILLIAM H. WOLF (1) remained in the West Division Fleet through 1910 and was then sold for use by others.

In 1903, Captain Sullivan expanded further in management of the Steamer WESTERN STAR for M. J. Cummings of Oswego, New York. This management lasted into 1911. The WESTERN STAR had a black hull with a white upper band around the entire hull and bow. The stack color was solid black.

The Chicago Navigation Company was incorporated in Springfield, Illinois in February, 1906 with $250,000.00 capital. Shares of this company were sold to friends and former associates of Captain Denis Sullivan with he and his wife being the controlling shareholders. The firm commissioned two steel bulk freighters to be built and these were delivered in 1906. They were named in honor of other shareholders in the company who were Messrs. James S. Dunham and William E. Fitzgerald. The DUNHAM was delivered June 6th and the FITZGERALD on October 10th by the building yards. Colors on the freighters consisted of black hulls with white cabins and all black stacks.

In 1907, a joint management agreement was executed between D. Sullivan & Company and Mr. Augustus B. Wolvin of Duluth, Minnesota. Under this agreement, ten vessels which Wolvin had constructed in 1903 were to be jointly managed henceforth. The ships were registered in the name of the Great Lakes & St. Lawrence Transportation Company. The names of these carriers were: Steamers JOHN CRERAR, H. G. DALTON, A. D. DAVIDSON, GEORGE C. HOWE, J. S. KEEFE, JOHN LAMBERT, ALBERT M. MARSHALL, S. N. PARENT, JOHN SHARPLES and ROBERT WALLACE. These vessels were of such size that they could readily operate to the lower St. Lawrence River through the existing canals of the day. It was D. Sullivan & Company's chore to help find eastbound cargoes for the ships, primarily from the industrial ports of Lake Michigan. Also in 1907, D. Sullivan was hired as manager of the then-new Steamer E. J. EARLING whose owner was the Franklin Steamship Company. This agreement was in place for 1907 only. Colors of the ships in both of the above fleet names were the same as those of the Chicago Navigation Company.

In 1908, the Gartland Steamship Company of Indiana was incorporated at Indianapolis with $600,000.00 capital on April 17th. Again, majority shares of the firm were in the hands of Captain Sullivan and his family and friends, including Marion Wolf. This corporate charter was administratively revoked by the Indiana Secretary of State on May 25, 1955.

Gartland Steamship ordered and took delivery of the steel bulk freight Steamer WILLIAM H. WOLF (2) in 1908 and placed the vessel in the iron ore, coal and grain trades. During 1908 D. Sullivan also took over management of the new Steamer B. F. BERRY for the Fremont Steamship Company and, also, the Steamer MANCHESTER. The BERRY was delivered from the building shipyard on June 4th and the firm managed it from that date. The latter vessel was acquired from the Inter-Ocean Steamship Company by the Milwaukee-Western Coal Company's steamship division. This firm was sometimes termed the Milwaukee-Western Steamship Company and was a wholly-owned subsidiary of the coal concern. The firm was dissolved by unanimous vote of the shareholders on December 30, 1940 following sale of all of the assets to Consolidation Coal Company in October, 1939.

Colors of the Steamers WOLF, BERRY and MANCHESTER in these early years were also the same as other vessels under D. Sullivan management except that the BERRY had a white "F" emblazoned on the black stack.

Management of vessels was expanded in 1910 when the Steamer CHARLES W. KOTCHER was taken over for the account of the Detroit Steamship Company. Its colors were black hull with white cabins and a reverse pennant beneath the name on the bow with a triangle logo on it. The stack was all black with the same reverse triangle logo in white and a raised small letter "D" upon the triangle.

The same year the Steamer CHRISTOPHER was added in behalf of the Christopher Steamship Company. The vessel had been delivered in 1901 to Mr. W. H. Meyer of Milwaukee and was his only steam bulk freighter. He did, however, operate his own tug fleet. The CHRISTOPHER's colors were the same as most Sullivan-managed vessels and its stack was all black.

On March 6, 1913, D. Sullivan & Company took ownership of the Steamer MERIDA for $65,500.00 in the name of the Edgewater Steamship Company. This carrier had been purchased by Edgewater at the auction of the Gilchrist Fleet and needed a manager for its owners who had little expertise in the business. D. Sullivan's reputation won it the management contract along with a majority ownership position. Edgewater colors were the same as other D. Sullivan managed fleets.

D. Sullivan's reputation for good stewardship won it the role of Receiver for the vessels of the defunct Chicago & Duluth Transportation Company in 1913. The carriers of that fleet included: Steamers MINNEKAHTA, MINNETONKA and MINNESOTA (2). The MINNEKAHTA and MINNETONKA were sold by Sullivan, as Receiver, to Mr. James Playfair of Midland, Ontario on February 26, 1914, but possession of the MINNESOTA (2) remained with the firm as Receiver.

During 1914, the company moved its headquarters to the former Continental and Commerical Bank Building on LaSalle Street in downtown Chicago. In 1915, it established a subsidiary firm called Lake Michigan Transportation Company for the purpose of owning and operating the Steamer MINNESOTA (2). This company and its only vessel remained in existence in D. Sullivan management only for the year of 1915.

The Steamer MERIDA was sold to Mr. James Playfair on September 29, 1915, leaving Edgewater Steamship with no vessel assets. Soon after, Edgewater was liquidated.

While vessels passed in and out of D. Sullivan management throughout its early years, the largest single management divestiture occurred in 1916 when the nine vessel fleet of Great Lakes & St.Lawrence Transportation Company (ships which began joint management for and with Mr. A. B. Wolvin in 1907) passed to French ownership due to World War I demands for tonnage on saltwater. It may be remembered that there were ten vessels in the joint management agreement of 1907. The Steamer JOHN SHARPLES had been previously sold and was not involved in this transaction. This nine ship sale was not without its anxious moments, however, because of the following events:

August 8, 1916:
Announcement was made of the sale of the nine ships through Ellwell & Company of New York City who were the brokers in the transaction.

August 31, 1916:
Federal Judge Landis granted an injunction prohibiting the sale on a petition filed by the Scranton Coal Company in District Court at Chicago, Illinois. The coal firm had a three-year contract with the fleet to

move coal from Oswego, New York to Milwaukee, Wisconsin and Chicago and it claimed default on that contract.

October 2, 1916:

An out-of-court settlement was agreed upon by which D. Sullivan & Company agreed to use substitute Great Lakes vessels to fulfill the shipping requirements of Scranton Coal for the duration of the contract. With this agreement to supply vessels to Scranton, the sale of the nine ships to the French went through and the carriers left the lakes later that fall.

A vessel passed into ownership in 1917, but D. Sullivan never operated the carrier. They had acquired the wooden bulk freight Steamer ROUMANIA on July 8th from the Reiss Steamship Company for the purpose of resale. The vessel was finally sold on August 10, 1918 to Captain William Nicholson with D. Sullivan acting as vessel brokers in the transaction.

Upon the death of Captain Denis Sullivan on October 1, 1918 at his home in Chicago following a long illness, another son, Harry, was elected to partnership in D. Sullivan & Company. Together with his brothers, another generation of Sullivans took command of the various activities of the family enterprise.

The bulk freight Steamer VINDAL was managed for the Calumet Steamship Company in 1921 and 1922, but it was not satisfactory for Gartland's needs and was sold out of the fleet early in 1923. The vessel's colors were: hull - black with white cabins; stack - all black.

Another short-lived vessel under the company's management was the steel bulk freight Steamer EDWARD U. DEMMER which was owned by the Milwaukee-Western Steamship Company. It was in the fleet in 1922 and began the 1923 season as well, but doom captured the vessel when it was sunk on May 20, 1923. The carrier had a black hull with white cabins and forecastle. Its stack was black with a wide yellow band, then a narrow black band, then another yellow band and black bottom.

In 1922, D. Sullivan took over management of two small, wooden freighters for the Kreetan Company. They were named MATHEW WILSON and O. E. PARKS and saw little service during that season. The major event of 1922 was the decision by the partners of D. Sullivan & Company to embark on a new and somewhat unique venture. In May and June of the year, three small "canal-sized" vessels were purchased from Empress Naviera of Cuba and the New England Fuel and Transportation Company. These were the former Steamers MINNEAPOLIS, ST. PAUL (3) and BRANDON. The two from Cuba were re-named BURLINGTON (2) and BENNINGTON (2), respectively. These three carriers had served on saltwa-ter during World War I, but had originally been lake ships which were capable of through navigation to the lower St. Lawrence River.

To facilitate this new venture, the partnership incorporated the Rutland-Lake Michigan Transit Company in Delaware with $500,000.00 capital and First Mortgage Bonds in the amount of $300,000.00. The vessels were typically called package freighters and were not constructed for the usual Great Lakes bulk freight shipments.

The idea behind this expansion was to join with the Rutland Railroad in making joint through water-rail rates to and from points in New England via the port cities of Ogdensburg, Oswego and Buffalo, New York to ports on the upper lakes such as Chicago, Illinois, Milwaukee, Wisconsin, Muskegon, Michi-gan and Duluth/Superior at the American Head-of-the-Lakes. In addition, any other port which could gener-ate sufficient tonnage to warrant a vessel stopping could also be served. Like most package freighters of the day, these ships had sideports in their hulls for moving cargo in and out of the hold and 'tween decks by handcart and cargo booms with steam winches to handle cargo out of the hatches. Typical cargo for these carriers would be bagged sugar and lumber eastbound and machinery and cotton piece-goods westbound. At first the business was a success, but it was not to be so for long. In order to regain the traffic they were loosing, the major trunkline railroads increased their rates to and from the port cities selectively to drive the traffic off the water route. Eventually, the business began to dry up, but that scenario will be related a little later in this story.

In the meantime, business was sufficient in 1922 to cause the partners to purchase two more, similar vessels for operation in 1923. These were the steel package freight Steamers BACK BAY and BROCKTON. They were both acquired from the Alaska Steamship Company with purchase dates of March 15th and May 1st, respectively. Like the vessels bought in 1922, these two ships also had been Great Lakes carriers prior to World War I and were, therefore, suitable for re-use in the lake trade.

All five vessels had dark green hulls and orange bottoms, with white cabins. The stacks were black with a broad white band and large black "S" placed in the center of the white band. Across the "S" was placed a stylized ribbon on which was printed, in white letters on the black ribbon, "RLMTC."

One other management arrangement was concluded for the 1923 navigation season only. That was management of the steel Steamer ALEX B. UHRIG for the Milwaukee-Western Steamship Company. The vessel was sold to the Reiss Steamship Company, along with the composite-hulled Steamer JOSEPH W. SIMPSON (formerly MANCHESTER) on November 6, 1923.

In 1926, the Chicago Navigation Company "swapped" their Steamer JAMES S. DUNHAM to the Reiss Steamship Company for their Steamer OTTO M. REISS (1). This was done on April 8th just as the carriers were fitting-out for the season. The swap came about because the DUNHAM had 9-foot hatch openings which were desirable for the coal trade and was five years newer. On the other hand, the OTTO M. REISS (1) was more powerful, had a greater carrying capacity by about 8% and also consumed more fuel. The difference in the ships' respective values to their managements was made up by Reiss "throwing in" some of its shares to D. Sullivan & Company.

The next few years were reasonably good in the grain and coal trades, but they began to wane seriously in the trades of the Rutland-Lake Michigan Transit Company. As will be disclosed shortly, this left Gartland bondholders with some hard decisions to make just about the time of the "market crash" of 1929. Perhaps the most significant decision was to merge all vessel activity into a NEW Gartland Steamship Company. This company was incorporated in Delaware on November 8, 1929 with an initial capital paid-in of $190,000.00. The total number of shares which were authorized for issuance was 30,000. Of this total, 15,000 were to be Preferred Stock and the other 15,000 shares were to be Common Stock without par value. The Preferred shares had a value of $100.00 each and the Corporation could redeem any or all of those shares on any dividend date by paying $102.50 in cash for each Preferred share.

The shareholders of Gartland Steamship Company of Indiana and the Chicago Navigation Company turned in their stock and their Rutland-Lake Michigan bonds and received 13,550 shares of $7.00 cumulative Preferred shares, no par value, but a stated value of $50.00 each and 6,775 shares of Common stock, no par value, but a stated value of $5.00 each. The total capital account in November, 1929 read thusly:

    Paid-In Capital   - $190,000
    Preferred Shares (13,550) - 677,500
    Common Shares (6,775) - 33,875
    TOTAL - $901,375

The onset of the Great Depression of the 1930's sealed the fate of Rutland-Lake Michigan Transit.

The business collapsed and Gartland Steamship, as principal bondholder, foreclosed and took the five ships into the fleet. The question was, what to do with the five additional vessels when the trades in grain and coal were already at a low ebb. Mr. Arthur C. Sullivan, Jr., the last president of Gartland when it was sold in 1969, suggests "management in those days must have been a pretty gutsy bunch." In any event, their foresight proved beneficial as they initiated a program to convert four of the carriers formerly in Rutland to steel, pig iron and scrap carriers with large hatches on deck. Three of these were fitted with fixed-base steam cranes. The BRANDON was converted to a self-unloader with a tunnel scraper. The BENNINGTON (2), BURL-INGTON (2) and BACK BAY were converted to crane ships and, formerly, the Gartland Steamer W. E. FITZGERALD was converted to a self-unloader at a cost of $109,000.00. The BROCKTON was fitted with three long hatches but no cranes were installed as she was used exclusively as a steel, pig iron and scrap carrier.

Before passing into the results of these adventures and intelligent management, it is interesting to note that in the 20-year period from 1908 to 1927, Gartland Steamship Company of Indiana and Chicago Navigation Company returned annually an average of thirty-one (31%) per cent on stockholder's equity! Dividends were paid out in substantial amounts, perhaps too substantial in light of what unforeseen develop-ments the 1930's would bring.

In 1933, Gartland acted as managers of the passenger Steamer ALABAMA. It had been bought on May 10, 1933 by the First Union Trust & Savings Bank of Chicago from the Referee in Bankruptcy Court. The operating company was named Journeys, Inc. Though the operation was originally planned for one year, it lasted through the navigation seasons of 1933, 1934 and 1935. The ship ran a regular schedule with passengers and automobiles between Chicago and Muskegon, Michigan with occasional extended excur-sion trips to Mackinac Island and Lake Superior. Public announcements were in the day's press in mid-June with the service to begin on June 30th. A total profit to First Union Trust, as Trustee for the Goodrich Line, was $80,000.00 for the three years, while that of Gartland, through D. Sullivan & Company, was $11,500 plus enough wild stories and anecdotes to entertain the successor management for years to come!

One such "wild story" regarding the ALABAMA and its master, Captain Amos Stufflebeam, was related thusly by Mr. Sullivan:
"Since the highways around Lake Michigan were both poor and highly congested, there was demand for this new service of the ALABAMA. After the bankruptcy of the Goodrich Transit Company, no such service as the ALABAMA offered was available.

Traveling salesmen, especially, found the ALABAMA a great convenience because they could relax on its six hour trip and be ready to make their calls in the Michigan hinterland once they disembarked in Muskegon, or vice versa if they were traveling to Chicago. The most popular and full bookings were during the summer months.

At this time, the "Century of Progress," Chicago's World's Fair, was also an attraction in that city. Site of the exposition was on what is now known as Meigs Field and Soldier's Field at the south end of Grant Park. Beyond, to the south, Jackson Park was also somewhat filled-in for added land space along Lake Michigan's shore. The exposition brought thousands of visitors to Chicago via the Steamer ALABAMA.

Besides travel convenience, the ALABAMA quickly developed a reputation for other "conve-niences." The period of prohibition was upon the nation at the time and "rum runners" from Canada were flourishing. In most instances, whiskey found its way aboard the ALABAMA, along with women and wa-gering. The former entered the United States at many points along the Detroit and St. Clair Rivers, then would be surreptitiously moved across Michigan for other distribution points. These features, though unad-vertised, made the ALABAMA even more appealing as the word spread.

On one occasion, two salesmen who had too much to drink before boarding the ALABAMA, were the first in line with their automobiles to drive aboard through sideports of the vessel. As the story goes, they were "so bombed" when they did drive aboard, they neglected to stop and, instead, drove right across the ship and crashed through the opposite sideport door, plunging into Muskegon Harbor. Both were drowned."

Someone might well ask where the money came from for all of the changes and reconstruction work which took place between 1930 and 1937 in the Gartland Fleet. In the first place, the entire fleet had been mortgaged to the Continental Bank in Chicago in the amount of $500,000.00. Also, the managers were successful in making a good profit in four of the Depression years. However, in two of those years, it was necessary to borrow additional funds from the bank in order to make interest payments. The Continental Bank really had no choice but to loan the funds as there was no market for their collateral (the ships). The bank did not panic, and the loans were fully repaid by 1940. Needless to say, there were no dividends paid to the Gartland shareholders during the Depression years and, by the time the $7.00 cumulative preferred dividend was resumed, the stock was in arrears $71.50 per share! Although net worth of the company was steadily increasing and payment of the preferred dividend was resumed in 1939, there was no effort to pay off the cumulative arrearage. This was taken care of by a corporate reorganization in 1960 and the company ended up with a single class of stock.

Beginning with the navigation season of 1935, Gartland chartered the Steamers J. J. H. BROWN and JAMES E. McALPINE from the Brown Steamship Company, and the Steamer RUFUS P. RANNEY (2) from the Tomlinson Fleet. While originally set for a one-year charter, the successful use of the vessels in the grain and coal trades led to the charters being extended each successive year through the navigation season of 1945. There was no change in the owner's markings on the vessels as these were demise charters with their owners supplying the masters and chief engineers as senior crew members.

In 1936, D. Sullivan & Company gave up the management of the Gartland Fleet. All of the shore personnel became employees of Gartland with the exception of those attached to the insurance department. Although the partnership continued until 1959 when it was incorporated as a firm of insurance brokers, it never again engaged in the management of ships.

Also in 1936, the Steamer BROCKTON was chartered to the Minnesota-Atlantic Transit Company for that season only. Meanwhile, Gartland chartered the Steamer F. D. UNDERWOOD from the Great Lakes Transit Corporation in mid-1936 and carried on the charter during the 1937 season. The vessel loaded 4,200 net tons of alumina at Ogdensburg, New York on October 26, 1936 for delivery to Milwaukee, Wisconsin and Chicago. The then-prevailing alumina price was $0.22/pound, making the cargo value about $2,000,000.00 and one of the most precious cargoes ever shipped up to that time on the Great Lakes.

On December 6, 1936, the Steamer BURLINGTON (2) was lost while attempting to enter the harbor at Holland, Michigan with 2,217 net tons of pig iron onboard. The cargo was destined for delivery to Lyons Construction Company of Whitehall, Michigan, but never reached its destination. The carrier stranded near the harbor entrance and broke up when trying to back off and became a total loss. Captain James Woods and his crew of 24 walked ashore the following morning. The vessel broke in two on the beach over the winter following the accident.

With the advent of World War II, demand for vessels on the "high seas" was very great. Under powers granted by Congress, the United States Maritime Administration was allowed to "requisition" ships from the Great Lakes for service on saltwater. Gartland's Steamers BACK BAY, BENNINGTON (2) and BROCKTON were so requisitioned and Gartland was offered $110,000.00 for the lot. After the war, a suit was filed by Gartland in the U. S. Court of Claims. The suit was settled twelve years later and Gartland was awarded the sum of $485,000.00 for the three vessels.

The Gartland Steamship Company acted as operator of the bulk freight Steamers AMAZON, S. B. COOLIDGE and COVALT for the War Shipping Administration beginning in 1944. These three vessels were operated by Gartland for varying lengths of time, namely: COVALT - in 1944 only, COOLIDGE - through 1947 and AMAZON until it went out of the operating agreement on December 31, 1949. During the navigation seasons of 1946 and 1947, the AMAZON and COOLIDGE served a large part of their operating time in the service of the Ontario Paper Company in the pulpwood trade.

Mr. Arthur C. Sullivan, Jr. has stated "The war years were hard on the company. For forty years the management kept clear of the iron ore trade, except for a brief interval in 1917. This trade was, and had been, dominated for years by the big mining and steel-producing companies who all operated their own ships. These vessels were large and most designed particularly for the ore trade. There was a constant conflict with the Lake Carriers' Association and the War Production Board who made every effort to force the small ships to carry iron ore at cheap rates under price controls. This was unreasonable because the small ships ended up carrying iron ore to points on the Niagara River and the Cuyahoga River. This was one reason that Gartland withdrew from the Lake Carriers' Association shortly after the war."

A change in senior management occurred upon the death of Arthur Clifford Sullivan, Sr., in Chicago on October 4, 1948. He had been president of Gartland and was succeeded on October 5th by Harry John Sullivan, his younger brother. This gentleman did not serve long as president because he died suddenly at his home in Winnetka, Illinois on January 27, 1950. His younger brother, and the youngest of five Sullivan brothers, served as president from then until Gartland's last president was elected on June 15, 1950 in the person of Arthur Clifford Sullivan, Jr. Arthur was president of Gartland until the company was sold in 1969.

Under Arthur's presidency, Gartland embarked on expansion moves which served the company and its shareholders well. The bulk freight Steamer FRANK E. TAPLIN was acquired from the Wilson Transit Company on October 24, 1950 at a cost of $450,000.00. The carrier had a cost of about $225,000.00 when built. It sailed on its maiden voyage April 11, 1908 with a cargo of coal from Lorain, Ohio to Ashland, Wisconsin. In 1953, Gartland bought the bulk freight Steamer JOSEPH WOOD from the Eastern Steamship Company which was managed by M. A. Hanna Company. This was a vessel which had a carrying capacity of 10,100 gross tons and which sailed on its maiden voyage May 25, 1910, light from Lorain, Ohio to Two Harbors, Minnesota to load a cargo of iron ore. Cost of the WOOD to Gartland was $600,000.00. Due to high grain rates and favorable tax regulations, the cash investment in both ships was recovered in just over three years! It should be mentioned that these newly acquired vessels were painted in the standard Gartland colors. The hulls were black with white cabins and red bottoms. The stacks were black with a broad white band and a large black "S" centered in the white band.

In 1956, the bulk freight Steamer HENNEPIN (2) was purchased from the Cleveland-Cliffs Steamship Company for about $250,000.00. It was operated as a straight-deck bulk freighter in 1956 while plans were formalized for its conversion into a self-unloader. That conversion work was completed in 1957. Prior to the conversion, a one-half interest in the vessel was sold to the Red Arrow Steamship Company, an affiliate of the Reiss Fleet of Sheboygan, Wisconsin. Redland Steamship Company was organized on January 11, 1956 in Delaware with 2,000 shares of no par Common stock being authorized. The HENNEPIN (2) was operated jointly with Red Arrow through a charter arrangement with the parent companies. The original officers included: Messrs. A. C. Sullivan, Jr. - president, W. W. Newcomet - vice president, P. D. Sullivan, Jr. - secretary and treasurer and W. A. Reiss, Jr. - assistant secretary and assistant treasurer. The original directors were: Messrs. Edmund Fitzgerald, W. W. Newcomet, Henry R. Platt, Jr., W. A. Reiss, W. A. Reiss, Jr. and A. C. Sullivan, Jr. One hundred of the authorized shares were issued in 1956.

The name Redland was derived from RED in Red Arrow and LAND in Gartland. Mr. Sullivan stated, "The ship was not only expensive to convert, but was singularly unsuccessful as a self-unloader and operational difficulties persisted until she was finally sold for scrap in 1975." The carrier's colors were identical to Gartland's except for the stack. It had a large red letter "R" centered in the white band.

The CLEVELAND NEWS announced February 2, 1956 that a new company had been organized by Gartland, Oglebay Norton and Federal Barge Lines. The firm was called Western Navigation Company and each of the three named firms held an equal amount of shares. Capitalization was $150,000.00 and the state of incorporation was Delaware. The purpose was to provide a terminal for the interchange of traffic between the Great Lakes and the Mississippi River system and to provide a well-located storage and loading facility for inbound traffic both from the lakes and from Western rivers. The facility was located on the Calumet River in South Chicago just lakeward of the 106th Street Bridge. Gartland provided local operating management and Federal Barge handled the sales and marketing effort along with Mr. John Kelly of Gartland. A warehouse was constructed on the property and sheet steel piling faced the dock for slightly over 1,000'. Seaway depth of 27-foot vessel draft was available alongside the dock. Pig iron, ferro-alloys and sulphur originated on the river as inbound cargo to the terminal. Scrap metal, structural steel and special grades of ore came into the terminal from the Great Lakes. Ocean vessels were handled to some degree, but only bulk material was accepted. There was no general cargo or container handling at Western Navigation.

In December, 1958, the Steamer HENRY R. PLATT, JR (1) was caught in the ice off Southeast Shoal on Lake Erie while enroute from Duluth/Superior to Buffalo, New York with a cargo of wheat. While the vessel made it to her destination and the cargo was undamaged, the vessel's hull had been so severely squeezed in the ice that she was declared a constructive total loss. The hull was sold for use as a storage grain barge in Buffalo harbor and remained there until being sold for scrap in 1966. This casualty loss, together with that of the Steamer BURLINGTON (2) in 1936, represented the two most severe losses in the Gartland Fleet's modern history.

A larger, replacement bulk freighter was purchased from the Pioneer Steamship Company on April 20, 1959. This was the Steamer G. A. TOMLINSON (1) and it was renamed HENRY R. PLATT, JR. (2) and began operating for Gartland in the spring of 1959. In addition, a friend and coal shipper, Henry L. Caulkins of Detroit, Michigan, decided to get out of the shipping business. Gartland purchased his Steamer RALPH S. CAULKINS on August 18, 1959. Mr. Caulkins controlled considerable coal traffic through his Waterways Navigation Company. The price of the ship was only about $100,000.00 and it began operating in the Gartland Fleet immediately. It was operated only a short period of time, however, as it was too small to be profitable, even in the domestic grain trade. It was sold for scrap in 1963.

It is noteworthy that all seven vessels in the Gartland Fleet in 1959 were active during the famous 100-day nationwide steel strike when most other fleets that relied upon iron ore for their cargoes had all or most of their carriers laid-up! It should also be noted that D. Sullivan & Company was incorporated in Illinois during 1959 after having been a partnership since its formation.

In the early 1960's, with the St. Lawrence Seaway open to large vessels, Gartland seized upon the idea of using its Steamer SULLIVAN BROTHERS (2) in Seaway service. Contracts of affreightment were signed with M. A. Hanna Company for westbound movement of iron ore from Sept-Iles, Quebec to Lake Erie and with this writer and Cargill, Inc. for the eastbound movement of grain from various Great Lakes ports to Baie Comeau, Quebec. Much of the grain forwarded was under Public Law 480 which is the U. S. Government's grain assistance program for export shipments. Since the grain under the program had to be moved in a U. S. flag carrier to the exporting terminal, a freight rate high enough for the SULLIVAN BROTHERS (2) to make some money on the voyages was affordable by Cargill, Inc. The vessel was fitted-out with a surface condenser so that her boilers would not be adversely affected by the salinity of brackish water in the river below Montreal, Quebec. Once this installation was made, the vessel remained largely in the Seaway trade for the majority of the 1960's.

A sidelight of this particular trading pattern was the excellent fishing it provided seamen aboard the SULLIVAN BROTHERS (2). All manner of saltwater fish were seen and many species were caught and eaten in the galley. When the sailor's luck was so good as to catch more than the crew could eat, the fish were frozen for later eating or for distribution to friends when the vessel would call at freshwater Great Lakes ports.

Due to a surge in demand for carriers to supply iron ore to Inland Steel's Dock #3 at East Chicago, Indiana, Gartland chartered the large Steamer EMORY L. FORD from M. A. Hanna Company on August 18th "for the balance of the 1963 season" and used her almost exclusively to move iron ore for Inland Steel.

On February 2, 1964, Gartland purchased the bulk freight Steamer H. L. GOBEILLE from the Cleveland-Cliffs Steamship Company for $250,000.00. The carrier was not operated in 1964 as the purpose of the acquisition was to convert her to a self-unloader. R. A. Stearn of Sturgeon Bay, Wisconsin was engaged to design the conversion, utilizing a number of engineering innovations which had been under study for several years. The Manitowoc Shipbuilding Company was selected to perform the conversion on a "cost plus" basis. The conversion was completed in 1965 and the carrier was renamed NICOLET. This carrier was the first built on the Great Lakes with a beam as great as sixty feet when commissioned in 1905. It was also the first lakes' conversion in which the cubic measurements of the holds were actually increased in the process. Cost of the work was $1,496,000.00 for which a five-year term loan was arranged with the Continental Bank. In this case, a sixty-year old vessel was given a "new lease on life." Its dimensions permitted it to operate profitably into many small ports for another twenty-five years. A few of the unique features incorporated into the NICOLET were its ability to unload cargo at 4,000 net tons per hour with only one man at the controls. Monitoring devices and the extensive use of hydraulics and remote controls were other features which were of state-of-the-art conception in 1965.

Also in 1965, the bulk freight Steamer THE HARVESTER was acquired from International-Harvester Company by the National Boulevard Bank of Chicago for $300,000.00 and was bareboat chartered to Gartland. A small floating contract for delivery of iron ore and limestone to Wisconsin Steel's works in South Chicago came in concert with the charter. The name of the vessel was changed to CHICAGO TRADER and it was operated in the Gartland Fleet through the fleet's sale. The form of financing noted above had been used for some years by life insurance companies to finance ocean vessels under U. S. flag and, later, to finance commercial aircraft. The CHICAGO TRADER had been well-maintained and was fairly fast for her age.

As a result of good demand for tonnage and the receipt of an iron ore contract in 1965, Gartland chartered the large bulk freight Steamer MERTON E. FARR from the Tomlinson Fleet Corporation for the 1965 season. Gartland also chartered the bulk freight Steamer J. CLARE MILLER from Columbia Transportation Company the same year and renewed that charter annually through 1968 as a partial replacement for tonnage Gartland was scrapping in those years. These two charters were the last which Gartland entered into prior to determining that further fleet operations would not be in their best economic interests.

Negotiations to sell Gartland Steamship Company, along with its subsidiaries, were entered into with Oswego Shipping Group of New York City. The group was headed by Mr. H. Lee White who had earlier concluded purchase of the American Steamship Company of Buffalo, New York. On March 1, 1969, the transaction took place which made Gartland and its affiliates a subsidiary of American Steamship Company. The sale to Oswego was made for $1,600,000.00 in cash. All shipboard personnel were continued on with their seniority maintained and all those members of the shoreside force were also continued if it was their desire to become part of the new organization.

Following the sale, D. Sullivan & Company was dissolved and its assets distributed to the share-holders. Gartland Steamship continued to exist as a subsidiary of American Steamship. This action ended nearly ninety years of Great Lakes operations and ownership by the Sullivan family.

As a matter of record, the five vessels which were sold to American in the transaction were the Steamers CHICAGO TRADER, W. E. FITZGERALD, HENNEPIN (2), HENRY R. PLATT, JR. (2) and NICOLET.

Under American's ownership, Gartland and Redland continued to exist until Redland filed a Certificate of Dissolution on March 23, 1976 and Gartland was merged into American on July 23, 1986 following a unanimous vote in favor of so doing on July 1, 1986.

Schooner-Barge ARMENIA (3)

This large wooden vessel was built for the iron ore trade, but did not enjoy a long life in that service. It was named for the Armenia Mine on the Menominee Range which opened in 1889 in the Lake Superior District. The carrier was active in Great Lakes trading until it was swamped and sunk in a severe storm near Colchester Reef, Lake Erie on May 9, 1906.

Steamer FRED PABST

Mr. Fred Pabst, of brewing family fame, was the namesake of this wooden bulk freighter. He had an investment posture in the West Division Steamship Company. His namesake remained active until October 11, 1907. At that time, it was involved in a collision with the steel Steamer LAKE SHORE in the St. Clair River and was badly damaged. Following the accident, the vessel was moored at Port Huron, Michigan until purchased "as is, where is" by a company which used the vessel as a lighter for some years.

Steamer WILLIAM H. WOLF (1)

Mr. William Henry Wolf was a principal in the West Division Steamship Company when his firm built this wooden bulk carrier in 1887. The shipyard was sold in 1890 and Mr. Wolf retired. He passed away on January 28, 1901. His widow continued active in steamship affairs for some years after his death. So far as is known, this vessel sustained no serious accidents while in the West Division Fleet.

Steamer WESTERN STAR

While under D. Sullivan management, this steel bulk freighter did not suffer any known major casualties. Under other operators it became a constructive total loss in Georgian Bay in September, 1915, but was salvaged after two years and returned to service. Namesake of this carrier, when named in 1903 by its first owner, Mr. Michael J. Cummings of Oswego, New York, was the fact that his other ships in his Red Star Line were of such size that they could trade throughout the Great Lakes. This vessel was too large to trade into Lake Ontario on which lake Oswego is located. Therefore, he named it WESTERN STAR because it could only serve on the WESTERN lakes.

Steamer JAMES S. DUNHAM

Captain James Sears Dunham was a friend of Denis Sullivan and the owner of the Dunham Towing & Wrecking Company of Chicago when this carrier took his name in 1906. He had been president of Lake Carriers' Association in 1897 and was president of the Chicago Navigation Company, original owner of this vessel. He also served as president of the Ship Owners' Dry Dock Company.

During its management period by D. Sullivan, the carrier sustained seven reported damages, as follows:

1. September 4, 1916:
Drawing 20'6" forward, 20'7" amidships and aft, the ship struck bottom at the foot of Lake Huron, about three-eighths of a mile above Lake Huron Lightship on the Point Edward ranges. At the time, the DUNHAM was going full speed and struck the bottom hard, first taking a list to starboard, then to port. Upon release and repairs, damage was not as great as might have been suspected from the impact. Repair cost was $3,557.94.

2. October 27, 1917:
A collision in Ashtabula Harbor, Ohio with the Steamer MARY C. ELPHICKE resulted in plate and internal damage of $2,267.89. Neither vessel was at fault and each paid for its own repairs as the two were maneuvering near the Pennsylvania Railroad Coal Dock.

3. November 5, 1917:
In fog, mist and heavy rain, the DUNHAM and Steamer ROBERT FULTON collided amidships by passing one another too close in the Detroit River. The DUNHAM was holed and sank. The FULTON was also badly damaged, but stayed afloat. Salvage and damage repairs to both vessels totaled $125,433.22.

4. June 13, 1919, 2230 hours:
The wheel of the DUNHAM struck some submerged object in the Canadian Canal at the Soo and damaged the hub while also breaking off one blade. The vessel was inoperable until emergency repairs were made to the extent of $5,813.06.

5. September 19, 1919, 0745 hours:
While proceeding up the Buffalo River and when abreast of the Lackawanna Railroad coal dumper, about 100' from that dock, the vessel rubbed slightly two or three times while moving slowly. She was drawing 19'8" forward and 19'4" aft at the time. Upon being unloaded of its grain cargo, the DUNHAM was inspected on drydock in Buffalo where repairs in the amount of $20,045.32 were found necessary. These were completed and the ship was returned to service on October 1st.

6. September 16, 1924, 0735 hours:
When drawing 19'0" forward and 18'8" aft, the DUNHAM struck an underwater obstruction while entering Buffalo Harbor. Site of the striking was one mile north of the main harbor entrance. Upon unloading a survey was commenced and it was found that repairs were needed in the amount of $19,293.17.

7. November 27, 1925:
This carrier collided with the Steamer CHARLES S. HEBARD in a snow storm in the lower St. Mary's River. Damage was more severe to the DUNHAM than the HEBARD as the DUNHAM was up-bound light and the HEBARD was downbound with iron ore. Both vessels were inspected and allowed to proceed on their courses. Later repairs to the DUNHAM amounted to $6,294.45.

Steamer W. E. FITZGERALD

The steel bulk freight Steamer W. E. FITZGERALD was delivered to the Chicago Navigation Company on October 10, 1906. It was equipped with a triple expansion engine which developed 1,467 shaft horsepower and two Scotch boilers. Each of these had a pounds per square inch pressure of 170 and a heating surface of 4,640 square inches. The boilers measured 13'9" in diameter and 11'6" in length.

Mr. William Edmund Fitzgerald was the namesake of this ship. He was killed in 1901 but had been a close friend of Denis Sullivan when he was a director and member of the executive committee of American Ship Building Company upon its formation. Captain Sullivan chose to honor his friend posthumously when this carrier was christened.

During its service in the management of this company, the FITZGERALD was known to have sustained seven recorded accidents, as follows:

1. April 24, 1918:
   The FITZGERALD and Steamer J. K. DIMMICK were working through the ice in Whitefish Bay when they collided. Damage was done to shell plating and internal frames which were bent by the impact on the FITZGERALD. The DIMMICK suffered only a few dented plates. Repairs to the FITZGERALD cost $9,881.60.

2. July 24, 1919, 0100 hours:
   The steamer was moored, bow upstream, at the Central Furnace Dock on the Cuyahoga River in Cleveland, Ohio and was loaded with iron ore to a draft of 20'7" all around. The carrier was about eight feet off the dock face in this position. After mooring, the FITZGERALD was approached by the Steamer HAROLD B. NYE in tow of the Tug LUTZ. The NYE's draft was 21' and she was touching bottom regularly in the mud. The LUTZ was barely assisting, with the NYE's engine doing most of the forward powering. As the bow of the NYE was abreast the stern of the FITZGERALD, the NYE's helm was put hard to starboard and the LUTZ began to pull off to port in order to assist the NYE around the sharp bend at that point in the river. Surging of the FITZGERALD occurred when the NYE was passing. Conflicting statements were given as to why the FITZGERALD's stern swung towards the NYE, but the collision resulted when the NYE was amidships of the FITZGERALD and the NYE avows that it was then going "dead slow." The matter was put before Mr. H. A. Kelley as Arbitrator in Cleveland, Ohio. His judgment was given on January 18, 1921, as follows:

   "I am of the opinion that the moorings of the FITZGERALD were sufficient to hold her to the dock save for the surge caused by the NYE's excessive force that was used as her engine was run full speed to overcome the muddy bottom. I do not concur that the lines of the FITZGERALD parted because they were in disrepair. It follows, therefore, that the NYE was solely at fault and is condemned to pay all the damages caused by the collision." Resulting repairs amounted to $13,885.09 to the FITZGERALD for the NYE's account.

3. September 23, 1921:
   The vessel stranded on Long Tail Point, near Green Bay, Wisconsin, while inbound with coal. The amount of $2,349.92 was expended to effect lightering of 710 net tons of coal to release the ship, then reload her so she could continue the voyage.

4. October 17, 1926, 0400 hours:
   A collision between the FITZGERALD and the Steamer COL. JAMES M. SCHOONMAKER occurred while the latter was lying at the "P.Y.& A." Ore Dock in Ashtabula, Ohio. The FITZGERALD was

entering the harbor and a strong northwest wind and current caused her to sheer to port and strike the SCHOONMAKER, damaging the bows of both vessels. Repairs were made afloat in the harbor. Those of the FITZGERALD amounted to $12,790.97.

5. December 14, 1926:

In crossing Lake Superior from Port Arthur, Ontario, the vessel encountered a severe gale and was badly shaken up. A total of 28,000 rivets required replacement when the carrier docked in Superior, Wisconsin. In addition, internal frames were bent and some plating was buckled. Cost of repairs was $37,122.33.

6. November 25, 1930:

The carrier stranded near Amherstburg, Ontario in the Detroit River while upbound with coal. The area is very rocky out of the channel and damage to bottom plates and internal frames amounted to $20,910.67.

7. April 25, 1948, 1700 hours:

A rare trip to Lake Superior was made by the FITZGERALD this date when it passed upbound with coal for Ontonagon, Michigan. In fact, it was the ship's only such trip to that time into Lake Superior as a self-unloader. Through an unfortunate set of circumstances of traffic above the Soo Locks, the vessel was forced aground by wind in order to steer clear of an impending collision with downbound traffic. Resulting damage to bottom plates and internals amounted to $10,997.80.

Steamer E. J. EARLING

This 10,000-ton capacity bulk freighter was named for Mr. Erastus Jonathan Earling who was also the namesake of the Earling Mine. He had a principal interest in the bituminous coal property located near Fairmont, West Virginia. His Logan Mining Company was a major forwarder of coal to Great Lakes ports when this ship took his name in 1906. During its brief time under D. Sullivan management, the vessel did not suffer any consequential incidents.

Steamer JOHN CRERAR

This canal-sized crane-equipped bulk freighter had a carrying capacity of 2,600 gross tons. Its three holds were evenly divided cubically and were each served by twelve-foot hatches on the deck. The vessel sailed on its maiden voyage August 4, 1903 with a cargo of corn and wheat from Chicago, Illinois to Quebec City, Quebec.

Namesake of this vessel was Mr. John Crerar who was a partner in the firm of Crerar, Clinch & Company of Chicago in 1903. The firm controlled the Equitable Coal & Coke Company, Searls Coal Company and the Duncan Coal Company for many years. Each of these firms was a large forwarder of lakeborne coal on the Great Lakes.

Steamer H. G. DALTON

This vessel was a sister-ship to the CRERAR and shared the same dimensions and capacity. Its namesake was Mr. Henry George Dalton who was a partner in Pickands Mather & Company when the ship took his name in 1903. In his position, he was able to influence much bulk cargo movement on the Great Lakes which was beneficial to this fleet.

Steamer A. D. DAVIDSON

The bulk freight Steamer A. D. DAVIDSON was one of four carriers in the 1903 building program for the fleet that was not crane-equipped. Its characteristics were the same as its sister-ships, however, and it operated over the same trade routes. Mr. Arnold Dustin Davidson was a practicing attorney and a friend of many senior men in the steel and financial circles of North America in 1903.

His namesake was sold for off-lakes use in 1916 and was renamed ARROMANCHES on saltwater. While on a trip from Montreal, Quebec to Cornwall, England, it was sunk by a torpedo from the submarine U-20 south of Ireland.

Steamer GEORGE C. HOWE

This crane-equipped vessel honored a cousin of Mr. Augustus B. Wolvin who held the title of Earl in England. His full name was George Augustus Frederick Lewis Curzon Howe. Only on rare occasions were all his names used. He became an investor in the Great Lakes & St. Lawrence Transportation Company on its formation and in other Great Lakes projects which Mr. Wolvin spearheaded.

While under management of D. Sullivan & Company, one accident is known to have occurred. That was on July 9, 1913 while the carrier was downbound with wheat in the Welland Ship Canal. The HOWE was in the area of Port Robinson, Ontario when she and the Steamer MAPLETON collided, doing slight damage to each other's bows. Repairs to the HOWE amounted to $3,292.09.

Steamer J. S. KEEFE

This bulk freighter was another of those built in 1903 without on-deck handling equipment. It was named for Mr. John Stoddard Keefe who was first vice president of the American Steel & Wire Company, with offices in Chicago, Illinois, when the vessel was named in his honor. His firm was a large exporter of metal products and used the vessels of this fleet for a considerable amount of those commodities moving to the eastern seaboard from the Chicago manufacturing district.

Steamer JOHN LAMBERT

Mr. John Lambert was vice president and a director of the Great Lakes & St. Lawrence Transportation Company when this crane-equipped bulk freighter took his name. He was also with the American Steel & Wire Company and took over as president of the firm during the period 1914-1916.

The carrier was sold for off-lakes use in 1916 and was renamed HOULGATE, but served on saltwater only a short time. On November 22, 1916 while on a trip from Montreal, Quebec to Havre, France with coal, it was hit by gunfire and scuttled twenty- three miles southeast of Owers, Isle of Wight, England.

Only one minor accident is recorded for the LAMBERT while in this fleet. That was a collision between she and the Steamer NORTH LAKE in the St. Mary's River on April 22, 1911. The LAMBERT was upbound in a narrow, ice-filled cut and the NORTH LAKE was downbound. The bow of the NORTH LAKE was finer than that of the LAMBERT and she was able to maneuver adequately in the slush ice, but had more difficulty in firm ice. On the other hand, the LAMBERT with its fuller bow had trouble in the ice under almost any set of circumstances. It was obvious to both vessels' masters that the pair could not safely pass in the narrow cut and the LAMBERT backed up, attempting to reach a wider part of the river. The NORTH LAKE, meanwhile, kept coming closer and blew a one-blast passing signal which was answered by the LAMBERT. When about 200' distant from the LAMBERT, the NORTH LAKE backed full speed but could not come to a halt before its bow sliced into the bow of the LAMBERT. Damage to the latter vessel amounted to $5,449.87 with only slight damage to the NORTH LAKE. Arbitrator Harvey D. Goulder ruled on December 28, 1911 that the vessels were mutually at fault and that each must bear its own repair costs.

Schooner-Barge ARMENIA (3) in the Soo Locks during the 1904 navigation season.

Steamer WILLIAM H. WOLF (1) in the 1890's.

Steamer FRED PABST being unloaded of a coal cargo at Milwaukee, Wisconsin in 1902.

Steamer JAMES S. DUNHAM as in the Chicago Navigation Company in 1909.

Steamer WESTERN STAR in a Georgian Bay harbor after being unloaded of a grain cargo.

Steamer JAMES S. DUNHAM in colors of Gartland Steamship while downbound in Little Rapids Cut, St. Mary's River, in 1924.

Steamer W. E. FITZGERALD as owned by the Chicago Navigation Company in 1910.

Steamer W. E. FITZGERALD in Gartland colors as a bulk freighter passing upbound in Little Rapids Cut, St. Mary's River, in 1927.

Steamer E. J. EARLING just after sea trials at Duluth, Minnesota on June 1, 1906.

Steamer A. D. DAVIDSON upbound in the St. Mary's River in 1910.

Steamer JOHN CRERAR downbound near the Soo Locks in 1907.

Steamer H. G. DALTON downbound below the Soo Locks in 1913.

Steamer GEORGE C. HOWE upbound near the Soo Locks in 1912.

Steamer J. S. KEEFE passing upbound above the Soo Locks during the 1915 navigation season.

Steamer JOHN LAMBERT downbound above the Soo Locks in early 1916.

Steamer ALBERT M. MARSHALL upbound in the St. Clair River in 1914.

Steamer S. N. PARENT passing downbound near Little Rapids Cut, St. Mary's River, in 1912.

Steamer JOHN SHARPLES passing upbound in Little Rapids Cut, St. Mary's River, during the 1913 navigation season.

Steamer ALBERT M. MARSHALL

Mr. Albert Mavlon Marshall was the namesake of this third bulk freighter in the 1903 series which was constructed without deck cranes. He was a friend and business associate of Mr. Wolvin's and the owner of A. M. Marshall & Company, insurance brokers for Great Lakes vessels.

The MARSHALL was equipped with a triple expansion engine which provided 650 shaft horsepower. Two Scotch boilers with 170 pounds per square inch of pressure each allowed a normal gait of ten miles per hour when loaded.

Only one accident befell the MARSHALL that has been recorded. That occurred on July 17, 1916 while the carrier was upbound in the Welland Ship Canal. It was approaching Lock 25 when it took a sheer and struck the rocky bank, bending four frames slightly and indenting plating. Repairs were made at Buffalo, New York at a cost of $2,339.28.

Steamer S. N. PARENT

Another of the "1903 class" vessels was the crane-equipped Steamer S. N. PARENT. It was named for Mr. Simon Napoleon Parent, the Premier of the Province of Quebec in 1903. He was honored because of the assistance he provided to this fleet when they were establishing an export base of operations in the port of Quebec City. His namesake sailed on its maiden trip May 6, 1903 when it departed Detroit, Michigan, light to Kelleys Island, Ohio to load stone for delivery to Duluth, Minnesota.

One incident of mishap is recorded for the vessel. It collided with the Steamer CITY OF OTTAWA on May 13, 1914. The PARENT was downbound and met the CITY OF OTTAWA in the upper level of the Cornwall Canal between Mille Rockes Bridge and the guard lock. The CITY OF OTTAWA got too close to the north bank and this produced suction which caused her to sheer across the canal and strike the PARENT on her port side abreast #2 hatch. Upper plating was dented on the PARENT, but she was able to proceed on her course to Montreal, Quebec. Repairs were made there to the extent of $4,653.55.

Steamer JOHN SHARPLES

The crane-equipped Steamer JOHN SHARPLES was delivered to this fleet by the building shipyard on August 30, 1903. It was equipped with a triple expansion engine and two Scotch boilers, each of which carried 240 pounds per square inch of pressure. The 650 shaft horsepower engine allowed normal speed of about ten miles per hour when loaded.

Mr. John Sharples was an export timber merchant and customer of this fleet with operations at Sillery, Quebec in 1903. Headquarters were located in the Union Bank Building in Quebec City. So far as is known, no significant incidents befell the vessel while under D. Sullivan & Company management.

Steamer ROBERT WALLACE

This fourth vessel in the 1903 group which was not equipped with deck cranes was named for Mr. Robert Bruce Wallace who was the president of the American Ship Building Company of Cleveland, Ohio. In the heyday of lakes shipbuilding, it was not unusual for a fleet to honor someone influential in a shipbuilding firm who may have had a direct or indirect interest in the financing of vessels being built. It is believed that Mr. Wallace had such an interest in some of Mr. Wolvin's carriers.

Steamer B. F. BERRY

The steel bulk freight Steamer B. F. BERRY was a carrier of 8,900 gross tons carrying capacity and its four cargo compartments were almost equally divided so far as cubic dimensions were concerned. It was under management of D. Sullivan from its initial trip through 1909 in behalf of the Franklin Steamship Company which was just being organized and staffed. In fact, a subsidiary firm named Fremont Steamship Company was the actual owner of this vessel with its home port originally being Fairport, Ohio.

Fitted with a triple expansion engine, the carrier also incorporated two induced draft Scotch boilers which each developed 180 pounds per square inch of pressure. The ship was delivered to its owner on June 4, 1908.

Mr. Benjamin Franklin Berry was the vessel's namesake. He was president of the Wills Creek Coal Company and the B. F. Berry Coal Company, both with headquarters in the Ford Building in downtown Detroit, Michigan. During its short tenure under D. Sullivan management, no incidents were recorded in the operation of this vessel.

Steamer MANCHESTER

As noted earlier in the story of this fleet, this composite-hulled bulk carrier was named in honor of the Manchester Trust whose beneficiary was Ella Gartland Sullivan. The 3,100 gross ton capacity carrier had three cargo holds which were served by seven on-deck hatches. During its service in the Sullivan fleet, two accidents have been noted which are as follows:

1. November 22, 1916:
While on a voyage from Buffalo, New York to Chicago, Illinois, the vessel lost her propeller while upbound in Lake Huron. The crankshaft was also cracked in the accident and considerable water damage was sustained in the engine room as a result of in-flowing water. While pumps were activated, they could barely keep up with the leaks. Upon drydocking in South Chicago, $9,661.47 was required in repair costs and replacement equipment, including a new wheel.

2. November 7, 1919:
The MANCHESTER hit an unknown underwater obstruction with her wheel while in the harbor at Buffalo, New York, sustaining damage to two propeller blades. Drydocking and repair charges at Buffalo amounted to $4,914.52.

Steamer JOSEPH W. SIMPSON

This is the same vessel which was just discussed, but with a different name. Mr. Joseph Warren Simpson was president of the North Western Fuel Company of Milwaukee, Wisconsin when this carrier was renamed for him in 1921. His firm was a major coal receiver of lakeborne coal cargoes from Lake Erie at the time.

During its time under D. Sullivan management with this name, two accidents are noted:

1. September 27, 1921, 1945 hours:
While shifting across the slip from the ore dock to the Lehigh Valley Coal Dock at Buffalo, New York, and going outside of the Steamer ANNA C. MINCH lying at the ore dock, a strong wind forced the bow of the SIMPSON to sag against the MINCH's starboard anchor and caused her to strand. Repairs amounted to $10,634.30.

Steamer ROBERT WALLACE downbound in the St. Clair River on an apparently hot summer day in 1910.

Steamer B. F. BERRY while upbound in the St. Mary's River in 1909.

2. November 14, 1922:

Navigating in strong winds and headed upbound, the vessel stranded on rocks near Tibbetts Point, Lake Ontario when loaded with shells from Ogdensburg, New York. The cargo was destined for delivery to Milwaukee, Wisconsin. Repairs at the end of the voyage amounted to $11,998.07 for bottom plates and internal framing plus replacement of 2,100 rivets.

Steamer WILLIAM H. WOLF (2)

Mr. William Henry Wolf of the Wolf & Davidson Shipyard in Milwaukee, Wisconsin was the namesake of this steel bulk freighter. This was the second carrier to bear his name and it was given this ship posthumously in 1908. Through the modern era of Gartland operations, this vessel was regarded as the fleet's flagship and its senior master was always appointed to sail her. It sailed on its maiden voyage June 6, 1908 with a cargo of coal from Lorain, Ohio for delivery to Milwaukee, Wisconsin. It was also the first vessel to load a cargo at the Rail-to-Water Transfer Corporation's coal dock at 102nd Street and the Calumet River in South Chicago when that facility opened on July 2, 1938.

During its more than fifty-five years of service in the Gartland Fleet, this carrier is known to have sustained eleven recorded accidents. These are noted, as follows:

1. April 27, 1913:

While working in ice about four miles from Buffalo, New York harbor, the WOLF and Steamer J. K. DIMMICK collided, causing appreciable damage to both vessels. Later surveys and repair costs amounted to $10,099.78 for the WOLF and a somewhat lesser amount for the DIMMICK. It was judged to be a "no fault" accident.

2. May 6, 1917:

The WOLF encountered heavy ice in the vicinity of Round Island, Lake Superior and did damage to both port and starboard plating and frames in the bow area. The vessel did not experience any leaks, however, and continued her upbound voyage. Later repairs were made to the extent of $2,612.20.

3 and 4. June 26, 1917:

Both accidents occurred on the same day! The first involved the WOLF and the Carferry Steamer MARQUETTE & BESSEMER No.2. While the former was lying at the dock in Conneaut, Ohio, the car-ferry broke adrift and struck the WOLF on her starboard quarter. The WOLF's repairs for this occurrence amounted to $3,613.69. The second accident happened while the WOLF was moving from the dock noted above to the No.4 Coal Dock in Conneaut, assisted by one tug on the bow line. A sudden heavy squall struck the WOLF while at the entrance to the slip. Both anchors were let go, but this precaution was not sufficient to prevent the vessel from striking the concrete dock face. Damage repairs amounted to $4,461.10 to the WOLF's bow, internal frames and plates.

5. April 28, 1918:

On this date, the Steamer FRANCIS E. HOUSE was lying at her winter berth in South Chicago, Illinois at the foot of 100th Street. On the 27th, the WOLF was placed alongside the HOUSE for the purpose of doing work by the local shipyard. Shortly after noon, the HOUSE was being towed from her winter mooring and in this maneuver the WOLF received some damage to her shell plating.

The master of the HOUSE had secured tugs for the purpose of going into the lake and shortly before he was ready to proceed, sent his mate over to inform the mate of the WOLF that he was going to shift his vessel. At the time, the wind was blowing very hard from westward and the mate of the WOLF objected to the shifting at this point. Notwithstanding this objection, the HOUSE shifted its position. The mate of the WOLF then let go his lines, but on account of the velocity of the wind, it was impossible for him to do anything but lay where he was.

Steamer MANCHESTER upbound in Little Rapids Cut, St. Mary's River, in 1918.

Steamer JOSEPH W. SIMPSON downbound in Little Rapids Cut, St. Mary's River, during 1927.

The master of the HOUSE claimed that the WOLF was making a "dock" of his vessel, and that the WOLF blew against the HOUSE in the severe wind that was then blowing. He also claimed that the WOLF did not handle itself properly in that her bow scraped against his chock when the WOLF was going astern and that the HOUSE was doing nothing unusual. This, however, was contested and sent to Arbitrator W. G. Stewart for a finding.

He found that the WOLF had done nothing illegal and that the HOUSE was at fault for not heeding reasonable caution in the face of the WOLF's objection and testimony. He awarded total damages for the repairs to the WOLF for the HOUSE's account which came to $9,888.90.

6. August 25, 1918:
The WOLF left the Northwestern Elevator in South Chicago in tow of the Tug WAUKEGAN. Just before arriving at Wisconsin Steel Company's dock, she sheered and struck the dock heavily. Damage was done to the stem and frames of the bow which totaled $4,846.07.

7. December 7, 1918:
While bound for Buffalo, New York from Milwaukee, Wisconsin, the vessel stranded on the southeast point of Southeast Shoal, Lake Erie. The WOLF required lightering to be released from its strand. It was loaded with grain at the time. Total cost of all required maneuvers amounted to $3,372.53.

8. October 14, 1920, 1710 hours:
Drawing 20'3" forward and 20'6" aft, the vessel rubbed bottom about 100' off the red gas buoy at the lower end of Woodtick Island in the St. Clair River. At the time, the WOLF was upbound with coal destined for delivery to Duluth, Minnesota. Cargo lightering was required, and then reloading after temporary repairs were made. Later repairs for this damage came to $15,679.64.

9. August 6, 1927, 1000 hours:
Making the turn at the Ohio Street Bridge in the Buffalo River, and drawing 19'7" forward and 19'9" aft, the WOLF's stern swung over into the corner of the channel and struck the dock. The WOLF's chief engineer claimed that her wheel stuck in a position that caused the accident. This was never disproved and the underwriter's paid $16,182.15 in damage claims.

10. September 20, 1928, 0840 hours:
When proceeding down the Maumee River at Toledo, Ohio, and between two railroad bridges, the WOLF's wheel struck an unknown obstruction. No damage was done to the ship other than the wheel and none to any shoreside facility. Repairs at the local shipyard cost $3,929.47.

11. April 26, 1931, 1145 hours:
Loaded with grain at Duluth, Minnesota and bound for Buffalo, New York, when drawing 18'4" forward and 18'6" aft, the WOLF found the wind fresh from the north upon departing Duluth. Snow squalls were encountered later while proceeding down Lake Munuscong, St. Mary's River and the vessel checked to slow speed. Nonetheless, it grounded on Hay Point Reef and required lightering of 43,000 bushels of grain to affect her release. After lightering, two tugs were required to make the vessel safely afloat. Cost of all these operations amounted to $28,729.22.

Steamer CHARLES W. KOTCHER

Mr. Charles Walker Kotcher was the namesake of this steel bulk freighter. He was the owner of the wholesale lumber company named C. W. Kotcher & Company in 1908. He was also vice president of the

Detroit Steamship Company and a director of the American National Life Insurance Company. The Kotcher Lumber yard in Detroit, Michigan was located at the foot of Adair Street and its offices were located on Gratiot Avenue.

This vessel was delivered by the building yard on March 4, 1908. It was equipped with a triple expansion engine and two Scotch boilers. Normal operating speed was ten miles per hour when loaded. It had a mid-summer draft carrying capacity of 7,300 gross tons. So far as is known, there were no serious accidents when serving under D. Sullivan management.

Steamer CHRISTOPHER

This steel bulk freighter was delivered to its original owner on October 14, 1901. The vessel had a 6,300 gross ton carrying capacity which cargo was typically spread evenly over its four cargo holds. The original owner was Mr. William Harold Meyer of Milwaukee, Wisconsin.

Namesake of the carrier was the son of Mr. Meyer. His father was manager of the Milwaukee Tug Boat Line in 1901. Like in the case of the Manchester Trust, actual ownership of the vessel was vested in the Christopher Trust of which the major beneficiaries were the Meyer and Starke families of Milwaukee. Lesser beneficiaries were Denis Sullivan and members of his family.

Steamer MERIDA

During its short tenure under D. Sullivan management, this steel bulk freighter is not known to have sustained any serious accidents, although August 10, 1913 an occurrence of record was noted. On that date, the MERIDA was coming down Lake St. Clair in the Grasse Point Channel when it sheered too close to the starboard bank and struck some underwater obstruction. It also struck shortly after when turning into the Windmill Point Ranges. Later it was found that the vessel had lost its rudder during the first encounter as well as its shoe. Later repairs in Detroit, Michigan ran to $6,846.16.

This carrier had three compartments in its cargo hold and they could accommodate a total of about 5,000 gross tons of iron ore or other dense cargo. It was equipped with a triple expansion engine and three Scotch boilers. Namesake of the ship was Merida, Venezuela, capital city of the state of the same name.

Steamer MINNEKAHTA

The steel Steamer MINNEKAHTA was a package freighter when under D. Sullivan management. It had been built as such and over the years variously engaged in both package freight and dry bulk trades for a number of companies. It was equipped with a triple expansion engine of 1,200 shaft horsepower and two Scotch boilers, each of which was capable of providing 160 pounds per square inch of pressure. The vessel's carrying capacity for dense cargo was 6,600 gross tons.

Steamer MINNETONKA

Like its near-sistership just mentioned, the steamer MINNETONKA was built with a triple expansion engine and two Scotch boilers. It was, however, built as a bulk freighter and did not become a package freight vessel until its conversion in 1911. It also bore a name of Indian origin as its namesake. Minnetonka is a western suburb of Minneapolis, Minnesota and was first settled in 1852. It now has a population of about 40,000.

Steamer MINNESOTA (2)

The iron-hulled Steamer MINNESOTA (2) was powered by a triple expansion engine. It was rebuilt with four Scotch boilers, instead of the original two, in 1911 when it became a combination passenger and package freighter. The namesake reference was to the state of Minnesota which was the 32nd state to enter the Union on May 11, 1858. The Chicago & Duluth Transportation Company had its northern terminus in the state.

Steamer ROUMANIA

The oak-hulled Steamer ROUMANIA was under D. Sullivan control as a broker with the intent of selling the carrier. Because of its rather restricted usability due to stress of weather damage in 1916, other owners did not flock to buy the carrier. Finally, Captain Nicholson bought her in 1918 with the intent of using her as a coal barge, but it is doubtful she ever saw such use for any significant period of time. The 91,700 square mile area in eastern Europe called Roumania was the namesake reference.

Steamer VINDAL

This small bulk freighter was managed for the Calumet Steamship Company by D. Sullivan following its return from saltwater service during World War I and somewhat thereafter. It was equipped with a triple expansion engine and two Scotch boilers which had been converted to operate in saltwater conditions.

The namesake reference came from the name of the owning company when the vessel was acquired from Moore-McCormack Steamship Company in 1921. The Vindal Company, Incorporated was located at 50 Broad Street in New York City and was a small trading firm providing odd-lot bulk transportation on the east coast for a short period of time in the early 1920's. Calumet Steamship Company management did not see fit to change the name during their brief operation of the carrier.

Steamer EDWARD U. DEMMER

Mr. Edward Uhrig Demmer was vice president and treasurer of the Milwaukee-Western Fuel Company of Milwaukee, Wisconsin in 1920 when this vessel took his name. The vessel was a typical bulk freighter with a triple expansion engine and two Scotch boilers. Carrying capacity was 6,800 gross tons in the carrier's hold which was divided into four separate compartments.

This vessel's only recorded accident was its last. She collided with the Steamer SATURN (2) at 0740 hours on May 20, 1923 in heavy fog forty miles southeast of Thunder Bay Island, Lake Huron, and sank in deep water. All twenty-five of the crew were rescued, twenty-four by the Steamer R. L. AGASSIZ and one by the Steamer JAMES B. EADS.

Steamer O. E. PARKS

The small bulk Steamer O. E. PARKS was constructed of wood and had a single cargo hold in which its 475 gross ton carrying capacity provided stowage for various products. The carrier was equipped with a steeple compound engine and one firebox. Its normal operating speed was about seven and one-half miles per hour when loaded.

Mr. Oscar Elmer Parks was the namesake of this vessel. He had sailed on the Great Lakes and commanded his namesake in the period 1903-1908. Concurrently, he owned a lumber mill in Michigan City, Indiana until he sold his interests in 1922 and moved east.

Steamer WILLIAM H. WOLF (2) passing downbound in the St. Mary's River in 1960

Steamer CHARLES W. KOTCHER passing outbound at Duluth, Minnesota in 1910

Steamer CHRISTOPHER entering the Soo Locks when upbound in 1922 with coal.

Steamer MERIDA downbound near the Soo Locks in 1913.

Steamer MINNEKAHTA passing downbound in the St. Clair River in 1913 when under D. Sullivan management, as Receivers for creditors of the fleet.

Steamer MINNETONKA as chartered by D. Sullivan & Company to the Mutual Transit Company,
upbound in the St. Clair River in 1913.

Steamer MINNESOTA (2) at Buffalo, New York prior to its departure for saltwater service in 1917.

Steamer ROUMANIA while operating in the Reiss Fleet, upbound at the Soo Locks during the 1917 navigation season.

Steamer MOOREMACK moored in the Hudson River at New York City in 1916 in this extremely rare photograph.
When taken, the vessel was undergoing conversion for saltwater service.
There is no known photograph of the vessel when named VINDAL.

Steamer EDWARD U. DEMMER passing upbound in Little Rapids Cut, St. Mary's River, during the 1922 navigation season.

Steamer O. E. PARKS in a rare photograph while underway with a cargo of pulpwood in 1925.

Steamer MATHEW WILSON outbound at Muskegon, Michigan about 1914.

Steamer MATHEW WILSON

This small wooden bulk freighter had a carrying capacity of 450 gross tonns in its single hold. It was used mainly in the pulpwood trade and its capacity for that course product was 4000,000 board feet. Its engine room was equipped with a steeple compound engine and one firebox.

Mr. Mathew Wilson was a prominent lumberman in western Michigan and an investor or director of numerous Michigan shipping concerns. He was one of the lakes' major shippers of lumber during the last decade of the 19th century.

Steamer BENNINGTON (2)

Bennington, Vermont was the namesake of this vessel. It was first settled in 1761 and was named for Benning Wentworth, the first royal governor of New Hampshire from 1741 to 1767. The carrier was so named in 1922 because of the community's importance to the Rutland Railroad. The 3,000 gross ton capacity carrier was powered by a triple expansion engine and was equipped with two Scotch boilers.

Steamer BRANDON

A quadruple expansion engine and two Scotch boilers powered this 2,800 gross ton carrying capacity package freighter. The vessel was named for Brandon, Manitoba which was originally called Brandon Station in 1881 when the Canadian Pacific Railway first passed through the site. Brandon is a rail center and distribution point.

During its time in the Gartland Fleet, the BRANDON is known to have sustained one serious accident. That occurred at 1257 hours on September 26, 1927 when the vessel was upbound with pig iron and coal. It ran on the rocks off Devils Island, Lake Superior and tore-up twenty-six feet of her bottom plating and bent internal frames. Her pumps were put in action immediately and the ship proceeded to Superior, Wisconsin which was not too far distant. There it was unloaded and drydocked with repairs costing $19,444.60.

Steamer BURLINGTON (2)

Burlington, Vermont was the namesake of this package freighter. It is on the mainline of the Rutland Railroad's former trackage and a city of about 38,000 population. A triple expansion engine and two Scotch boilers provided power for this carrier.

While serving as a package freighter, the BURLINGTON (2) suffered one major damage. On August 12, 1927, laden with grain, the vessel sank in the harbor at Montreal, Quebec. The sinking was caused because someone erroneously removed a seacock cover instead of removing a pump cover. A large part of the cargo was damaged. The underwriters awarded a salvage contract to Sorel Mechanical Shops of Montreal on August 15th. The ship was refloated and placed on drydock at Montreal on August 30th. The rudder, shoe and thirteen bottom plates required replacement. Total cost of the salvage and repairs was $16,188.35.

Following conversion to a crane-equipped bulk freighter in 1929, the vessel sustained two more serious accidents. The first happened on October 7, 1930 at 0300 hours. The ship ran aground on rocky bottom about one mile due east of Cudahy, Wisconsin in dense fog on Lake Michigan. The Tug WELCOME and two derrick barges with air compressors were sent to the scene from Milwaukee on the 8th and began their work. At the time, the BURLINGTON (2) had 3,050 net tons of finished steel onboard. After about 1,000 tons was lightered, release was accomplished on November 4th. The vessel was towed back to South

Chicago, Illinois and was placed on drydock where repairs were effected. One hundred twelve bottom plates needed replacing, along with internal framing, rivets, etc. at a cost of $49,076.14.

The second accident as a crane vessel was the BURLINGTON's last. On December 6, 1936 she was loaded with a cargo of pig iron amounting to 2,217 net tons. It had been put aboard in Toledo, Ohio and was destined for delivery to Holland, Michigan for the Lyons Construction Company. The cargo was valued at $45,000.00. The BURLINGTON (2) encountered difficulty making the Holland harbor entrance and stranded. The crew of 24 were saved but the vessel broke in two with a jagged fisure 18" wide running from her deckline to the water on the starboard side and a narrower rupture down the port side. This damage occurred by December 8th and heavy winter weather and storms doomed the vessel to scrap.

Steamer ALEX B. UHRIG

Mr. Alexander Bernhard Uhrig was vice president of the Milwaukee-Western Fuel Company when this ship took his name in 1919. A triple expansion engine and two Scotch boilers provided power for his namesake.

Only one major accident befell the UHRIG in the Gartland Fleet. On June 4, 1923, she stranded at Bailey's Harbor, Wisconsin in foggy weather. Lightering, towing to Manitowoc, Wisconsin and repairs cost $38,769.47.

Steamer BACK BAY

The 3,000 gross ton carrying capacity package freight Steamer BACK BAY was launched January 21, 1908. It was equipped with a quadruple expansion engine and two Scotch boilers in its engine room. The namesake reference was the Back Bay area of Boston, Massachusetts. It is notable that the vessel was the first to carry merchandise from the Pacific Coast of the United States via the Mississippi River to Chicago, Illinois. It completed that voyage on June 9, 1923 when the vessel arrived at Chicago from Seattle, Washington.

Shortly after making this trip to Chicago, the BACK BAY stranded on Beaver Island, Lake Michigan when upbound from Chicago and Milwaukee to Buffalo, New York with a cargo of pig iron. Sixty bottom plates and internal frames were badly damaged in the grounding. Repairs were made at Manitowoc, Wisconsin to the extent of $29,654.70. This was the carrier's only major accident as a package freighter.

After conversion to a crane-equipped bulk carrier in 1924, three more incidents of damage are noted, as itemized below:

1. May 14, 1929:
The vessel stranded on Pilot Island, 117 miles southeast of Plum Island on the northeast side of Lake Michigan's entrance to Porte des Morts Passage. Damage was done to twelve bottom plates, the lower forepeak and frames. Following release on May 17th, repairs were made at Manitowoc in the amount of $8,377.90.

2. July 14, 1930, 0730 hours:
While upbound with a cargo of salt for delivery to Duluth, Minnesota, the BACK BAY struck a bridge pier above the Soo Locks and tore a large hole in her port side below the waterline. As the vessel was taking on water rapidly, the master beached the boat about one mile upriver. Divers investigated the damage

on July 15th and put a temporary patch in place so that the BACK BAY could continue its voyage. Following unloading, the vessel was drydocked at Superior, Wisconsin on July 17th. It was repaired at a cost of $11,767.41 and was loaded with grain and on its way out of the harbor on July 29th.

3. May 26, 1938:

      The BACK BAY collided with the Steamer EMPEROR off Southeast Shoal, Lake Erie in foggy weather. The vessel proceeded with caution to drydock at Lorain, Ohio where repairs were made to the starboard side shell abreast hatches #2, 3 and 4. Total cost of repairs came to $21,007.64.

Steamer BROCKTON

      The Steamer BROCKTON was very similar to the other "canal-sized" vessels in the fleet, being equipped with a quadruple expansion engine and two Scotch boilers in her engine room. Namesake of this carrier was an industrial city in Plymouth County, Massachusetts, about twenty miles south of Boston. So far as is known, the Steamer BROCKTON did not suffer any major reported damages while in the Gartland Fleet.

      The BROCKTON set some sort of "long load" record on November 18, 1940 when she cleared the Lehigh Valley Railroad Dock in Buffalo, New York with a cargo of 2,500 gross tons of spiegelsen ore for delivery to Indiana Harbor, Indiana. What was unusual was that the cargo was loaded by buckets swung aboard, much akin to loading methods 60-70 years earlier.

      The two dock magnets lacked sufficient power to handle the material which was in the form of pig iron. The ore had a high manganese content and was generally used in the Bessemer process of steelmaking. The cargo had been brought to Buffalo by rail from Palmerton, Pennsylvania.

      A gang of 43 men was required to fill the buckets before they were picked up by cranes and swung into the BROCKTON's hold. The men picked up the bars by hand and loaded the buckets. About thirty hours was needed to accomplish the transfer from dock to vessel.

Steamer OTTO M. REISS (1)

      The steel bulk freight Steamer OTTO M. REISS (1) details were provided for the same vessel in the Reiss Fleet. Mr. Otto Martin Reiss was the carrier's namesake.

Steamer W. E. FITZGERALD

      Details of this vessel were provided earlier in the Gartland Fleet story. It is mentioned again to show her configuration following her 1928 conversion.

Steamer SULLIVAN BROTHERS (1)

      This bulk freighter is the same one noted when it was named OTTO M. REISS (1). Its namesakes were Messrs. Arthur, Harry, Frank and Paul Sullivan, all of whom were partners in D. Sullivan & Company. While serving under this name, the carrier was not known to have suffered serious mishaps.

Steamer ALABAMA

This passenger steamer was launched December 18, 1909 and originally was a unit of the Goodrich Transit Company. That firm operated numerous package freight and passenger carriers, primarily on Lake Michigan, and named its vessels for various states. In this case, the state of Alabama was honored. The ship's hull was specially strengthened for ice operation. Following bankruptcy of the Goodrich Transit Company, the vessel was purchased by creditors and operated by Gartland during 1933, 1934 and 1935. During these years, the carrier is not known to have sustained any serious mishaps.

Steamer J. J. H. BROWN

The bulk Steamer J. J. H. BROWN was named for Mr. James Jeremiah Hezekiah Brown, an early pioneer in Great Lakes shipping and founder of the Brown Steamship Company and associated firms of Buffalo, New York. His namesake was delivered by the building shipyard on May 12, 1908 and entered the iron ore, coal and grain trades. It was equipped with a triple expansion engine which developed 1,500 shaft horsepower and two Scotch boilers. Each of the boilers carried 170 pounds per square inch of pressure.

While the carrier was involved in numerous adventures under its owner's management, none were noted while operating under charter to Gartland Steamship.

Steamer JAMES E. McALPINE

Mr. James Ernest McAlpine was this bulk freighter's namesake. He was president of the firm of Brown & Rogers of Buffalo, New York and Shasta Steamship Company when this vessel took his name in 1934.

This vessel was a sistership to the BROWN just noted above. It was delivered by the building shipyard on May 17, 1908. During its charter to the Gartland Fleet, no known mishaps befell the vessel.

Steamer RUFUS P. RANNEY (2)

Mr. Rufus Percival Ranney, vessel financier of this vessel built for the Triton Steamship Company, was the carrier's namesake. It was very similar to the two above-named vessels, was useful in the grain trade and chartered by the Gartland Fleet for that purpose. It is not known to have sustained any serious mishaps while under charter to Gartland.

Motor Vessel ORMIDALE

This World War I bulk carrier was only in the Gartland Fleet, under bareboat charter, from July through December 1935. Gartland paid a fee of $775.00 per month for use of the vessel to its owner, Motorship Transit Company. This was a partnership of Captain John Roen of Sturgeon Bay, Wisconsin and Captain Louis Larson of Marinette, Wisconsin. The ship's operation was mainly for use in hauling pig iron and rip-rap stone for two construction projects. During this service, no ill fate befell the carrier except on October 30, 1935. On this date, it collided with the Norwegian Steamer VIATOR ten miles south of Thunder Bay Island, Lake Huron. The ORMIDALE was downbound from Duluth, Minnesota to Buffalo, New York and the VIATOR was upbound for Chicago, Illinois. The ORMIDALE struck the VIATOR amidships in the area of engine and cabins with the engine room flooding immediately. The ORMIDALE held her prow in the gash until the VIATOR's crew could climb safely aboard the ORMIDALE. The latter then backed away, leaving the saltwater vessel to sink shortly afterwards. Investigation into the accident concluded that confusion as to Great Lakes Rules of the Road were abrogated by the VIATOR and the ORMIDALE was held blameless in the accident.

Steamer F. D. UNDERWOOD

The Steamer F. D. UNDERWOOD was chartered by Gartland for the period June-December 1936. In that brief time, Arthur Sullivan recalls that its temperamental triple expansion engine gave the chief engineer "operating fits" aboard the vessel. He noted, "The chief engineer used to open the pitcocks and put raw ether into each cylinder to prime it. Then the crew would leave the ship while the engine was started and they would watch it belch and smoke until it was felt safe to return." It must have been quite a sight to see the crew scramble to nearby bollards and sit there until given the "all clear" to reboard!

Namesake of this carrier was Mr. Frederick Douglas Underwood who was president of the Erie Railroad in 1910 when this vessel took his name.

Steamer AMAZON

Namesake of this vessel was the Amazon River of South America, largest river in the world. The ship was chartered from the United States Government during the period 1944-1949 and is not known to have sustained any serious damages during that time.

Steamer S. B. COOLIDGE

Equipped with a triple expansion engine and two Scotch boilers, this vessel was a typical bulk freighter when powered from a barge in 1902. It had three cargo compartments and a carrying capacity of 5,700 gross tons. The carrier was named for Mr. Sollace Burroughs Coolidge when renamed in 1925. At that time, Mr. Coolidge was vice president of the Clarkson Coal & Dock Company.

Steamer COVALT

This bulk carrier was originally built under contract for the United States Government. By the time it was delivered, World War I was over and the ship was no longer needed in government service. It was acquired by the Morton Salt Company and served them until being chartered to Gartland. The vessel was equipped with a triple expansion engine which developed 1,250 shaft horsepower, and two Scotch boilers. Each of these carried 175 pounds of pressure per square inch.

Steamer FRANK E. TAPLIN

Mr. Frank Elijah Taplin was president and principal owner of the Cleveland & Western Coal Company when this bulk freighter took his name in 1920. By 1925, he was the largest individual coal shipper on the Great Lakes. During its career in the Gartland Fleet, this 7,400 gross ton capacity carrier is not known to have suffered any serious mishaps. The vessel was equipped with a triple expansion engine and two Scotch boilers and was originally delivered on March 4, 1908.

Steamer JOSEPH WOOD

Captain Joseph Sutherland Wood was the namesake of this carrier when it was originally delivered by the building shipyard on May 23, 1910. Captain Wood was the senior captain in the Wilson Transit Fleet in 1910 and a relative of Thomas Wilson. This 9,500 gross ton carrying capacity bulk freighter was equipped with a triple expansion engine and two Scotch boilers. Normal operating speed was eleven miles per hour when loaded.

Steamer SULLIVAN BROTHERS (2)

Namesakes of this carrier were the same as earlier noted for the Steamer SULLIVAN BROTH-ERS (1). This ship's characteristics are the same as the vessel just noted because it is the same vessel, having been given its last name in 1957.

Steamer HENRY R. PLATT, JR. (1)

This bulk freighter was equipped with a quadruple expansion engine and two Scotch boilers, each of which carried 250 pounds of pressure per square inch. Shaft horsepower of the carrier was 1,700. The only serious accident to the vessel when operating under this name in the Gartland Fleet was the ice-crushing damage on Lake Erie which doomed the vessel to storage barge service in Buffalo, New York beyond 1958.

Mr. Henry Russell Platt, Jr. was the carrier's namesake. He was treasurer of the Truax-Traer Coal Company when this vessel took his name in 1957.

Steamer HENNEPIN (2)

This 9,500 gross ton carrying capacity bulk freighter was equipped with a triple expansion engine and two Scotch boilers. The vessel's namesake was Father Jean Louis Hennepin, a member of La Salle's expedition in 1678 in search of the Mississippi River.

Steamer HENRY R. PLATT, JR. (2)

The keel for this carrier was laid May 13, 1909 and it was launched July 10th. Delivery to its original owner was made by the shipyard on August 9th. The vessel was equipped with a triple expansion engine which developed 1,760 shaft horsepower at 83 revolutions per minute. Two Scotch boilers each carried 180 pounds of pressure per square inch. The American Bureau of Shipping surveyor's report at fit-out stated: "We consider this vessel a good risk in every way."

Mr. Henry Russell Platt, Jr. was the namesake as he was for the earlier Gartland ship which bore the name.

Steamer RALPH S. CAULKINS

Mr. Ralph Stone Caulkins was a son of Henry L. Caulkins, president of the Waterways Navigation Company of Detroit, Michigan. The senior Caulkins named this steel bulk freighter for Ralph soon after he graduated from Yale University and entered the employ of the Canadian Furnace Company at Port Colborne, Ontario.

This steamer was equipped with a triple expansion engine of 1,480 shaft horsepower and two Scotch boilers of 170 pounds per square inch pressure each. Normal operating speed in the loaded condition was twelve miles per hour.

Steamer BENNINGTON (2) at Milwaukee, Wisconsin in 1923 as a combination bulk and package freighter.

Steamer BENNINGTON (2) underway as a crane vessel in the early 1940's.

Steamer BRANDON in 1926 as a package freighter at Milwaukee, Wisconsin.

Steamer BRANDON in
the Detroit River as a
self-unloader with
its unique
86' boom in
the late 1920's.

Steamer BURLINGTON (2) as a package freighter in 1926.

Steamer BURLINGTON (2) downbound in Little Rapids Cut, St. Mary's River, as a crane ship in 1929.

Steamer ALEX B. UHRIG passing downbound in Little Rapids Cut, St. Mary's River, in 1923.

Steamer BACK BAY leaving Chicago, Illinois as a package freighter in 1923.

Steamer BACK BAY as a crane vessel while underway on Lake St. Clair in the early 1940's.

Steamer BROCKTON, in a very rare photograph, as a package freighter in 1923.

Steamer BROCKTON as a bulk freighter abreast Marine City, Michigan, in the St. Clair River, on April 13, 1941.

Steamer OTTO M. REISS (1) passing upbound in Little Rapids Cut, St. Mary's River, in 1929.

Steamer W. E. FITZGERALD as a self-unloader upbound in the St. Mary's River on July 31, 1962.

Steamer SULLIVAN BROTHERS (1) being unloaded in Buffalo, New York in 1955.

Steamer ALABAMA in a very rare photograph, as managed by Gartland in 1934.

Steamer J. J. H. BROWN as chartered by Gartland, underway in 1944.

112

Steamer JAMES E. McALPINE upbound in the Detroit River while under charter to Gartland in 1936.

Steamer RUFUS P. RANNEY (2) downbound at the Soo Locks in 1941 while under charter to the Gartland Fleet.

Steamer EMORY L. FORD

This bulk freighter was built on the Isherwood hull design of longitudinal framing. Vessels so designed normally had a greater carrying capacity at any given draft than any similarly-sized counterpart. The vessel was delivered to its original owner on August 26, 1916 and sailed on its maiden voyage the same day, light from Lorain, Ohio to Marquette, Michigan to load iron ore. The FORD loaded 487,325 bushels of corn at Duluth, Minnesota on June 22, 1922 for delivery to Depot Harbor, Ontario to set a new Great Lakes record for that commodity. It also set a new record for barley cargoes on December 9, 1929 when it took on 542,076 bushels at Fort William, Ontario for Buffalo, New York delivery.

The carrier had a vertical triple expansion engine, three cylinders and three Scotch boilers. Each boiler carried a pressure of 180 pounds per square inch.

Gartland Steamship chartered this vessel for about the last half of the 1963 navigation season due to the fleet's need for added carrying capacity. The namesake of the vessel was Mr. Emory Leyden Ford. He was vice president of the Michigan Alkali Company of Detroit, Michigan when the ship took his name in 1916. Michigan Alkali had been founded by this grandfather, Captain J. B. Ford.

Steamer CHICAGO TRADER

The bulk freight Steamer CHICAGO TRADER was so named because of the headquarters city of Gartland Steamship being in Chicago, Illinois. Additionally, the ship traded in numerous Great Lakes areas. Finally, Mr. Arthur C. Sullivan, Jr. was registered to trade and was a member of the Chicago Board of Trade.

This carrier was delivered to its original owner on August 20, 1911 and sailed on its first trip, upbound with coal from Lorain, Ohio to Duluth, Minnesota on August 21st. On September 23, 1921, the vessel set a Great Lakes record for corn cargoes when it loaded 432,980 bushels at Milwaukee, Wisconsin for Port McNicoll, Ontario delivery. The vessel was equipped with a triple expansion engine and two Scotch boilers. Horsepower was rated at 1,800 and the boilers each carried 180 pounds per square inch of pressure.

Steamer MERTON E. FARR

This bulk freighter served in the Gartland Fleet only under charter during the navigation season of 1965. It was named for Mr. Merton Emerson Farr, president of the Detroit Shipbuilding Company when the carrier was constructed. Shortly before being completed, the vessel was sold to Zenith Steamship Company, one of Mr. G. A. Tomlinson's enterprises. That firm did not see fit to change the name. Delivery date to Zenith was October 17, 1920.

The vessel was powered by a triple expansion engine of 2,300 shaft horsepower and three Scotch boilers with 185 pounds per square inch of pressure in each. This engine room equipment was built in Lorain, Ohio, then shipped to Wyandotte, Michigan for installation.

Steamer J. CLARE MILLER

The bulk freight Steamer J. CLARE MILLER was delivered to its first owner on May 6, 1906 and had a triple expansion engine of 1,760 shaft horsepower rating. It also had two Scotch boilers with pressure of 180 pounds per square inch. The carrier was under charter in the Gartland Fleet during the navigation seasons of 1965-1968, inclusive. The carrier established two new port records on the same trip in 1907 when it loaded 10,387 net tons of coal at Lorain, Ohio on October 9th for unloading at Gladstone, Michigan. It was the largest coal cargo ever handled at either port up to that time.

Mr. James Clare Miller, vice president or raw materials for Armco Steel Corporation, was the namesake of this carrier when it took his name in 1937.

Steamer NICOLET

This vessel was the first to be built with a 60-foot beam when it was launched in 1905. It was named for the French explorer Jean Nicolet who came to Canada with Samuel de Champlain in 1618. After the Gartland Fleet was sold to American Steamship Company, that firm later repowered the carrier, already almost seventy years old, and the ship still exists on the lakes, although it has been laid-up for a few years.

Motor Vessel ORMIDALE downbound in connecting channels with a cargo of rip-rap stone.

Steamer F. D. UNDERWOOD during 1936-1937 winter lay-up following charter to the Gartland Fleet.

Steamer AMAZON upbound in the St. Clair River when chartered by Gartland in 1948.

Steamer S. B. COOLIDGE downbound in the St. Clair River when chartered by Gartland on August 26, 1945.

Steamer COVALT under charter to the Gartland Fleet shown leaving Chicago, Illinois on August 22, 1943.

Steamer FRANK E. TAPLIN downbound in the St. Mary's River on September 15, 1962.

Steamer JOSEPH WOOD in Gartland colors passing downbound in the St. Clair River in 1953.

Steamer SULLIVAN BROTHERS (2) passing downbound in Little Rapids Cut, St. Mary's River, on August 19, 1957.

Steamer HENRY R. PLATT, JR. (1) at Victory Soya Mills Elevator in Toronto, Ontario on July 11, 1958.

Steamer HENNEPIN (2) in its only season as a bulk freighter in the Gartland Fleet, upbound in the Detroit River in 1956.

Steamer HENNEPIN (2) as a self-unloader at Dock #24 in Cleveland, Ohio on June 18. 1959.

Steamer HENRY R. PLATT, JR. (2) upbound in Sault Ste. Marie Harbor on September 14, 1963.

Steamer RALPH S. CAULKINS downbound on Lake Huron on August 8, 1960.

Steamer EMORY L. FORD as chartered by Gartland, in a very rare photograph, passing
upbound in Little Rapids Cut, St. Mary's River, on August 28, 1963.

Steamer CHICAGO TRADER passing upbound in Little Rapids Cut, St. Mary's River, on July 5, 1965.

Steamer MERTON E. FARR while under charter to Gartland in 1965.

Steamer J. CLARE MILLER, as chartered by the Gartland Fleet, passing downbound
in Little Rapids Cut, St. Mary's River, on September 15, 1968.

Steamer NICOLET while passing downbound on Lake Huron on October 30, 1966.

STATISTICAL AND OTHER PERTINENT INFORMATION FOR VESSELS OF THE GARTLAND STEAMSHIP COMPANY AND ITS AFFILIATES

Schooner-Barge ARMENIA (3)
    Built: James Davidson Shipyard, West Bay City, Michigan - 1896
    Hull No.: 73
    Overall Dimensions: 298' x 44' x 21'7"
    Years in D. Sullivan Fleet: 1902-1906
    Official Number: U. S. 107219
    Other: Swamped and sunk in severe storm near Colchester Reef, Lake Erie on May 9, 1906.

Steamer FRED PABST
    Built: Wolf & Davidson Shipyard, Milwaukee, Wisconsin - 1890
    Hull No.: None assigned
    Overall Dimensions: 302' x 42' x 29'
    Years in D. Sullivan Fleet: 1902-1907
    Official Number: U. S. 120794
    Other: Collided October 11, 1907 with Steamer LAKE SHORE in the St. Clair River. Thereafter, decommissioned "for non-transportation use," with engine removed. Abandoned in 1920.

Steamer WILLIAM H. WOLF (1)
    Built: Wolf & Davidson Shipyard, Milwaukee, Wisconsin - 1887
    Hull No.: None assigned
    Overall Dimensions: 300' x 39'4" x 23'3"
    Years in D. Sullivan Fleet: 1902-1910
    Official Number: U. S. 81164
    Other: Destroyed by fire October 20, 1921 abreast Marine City, Michigan in St. Clair River.

Steamer WESTERN STAR
    Built: Detroit Shipbuilding Company, Wyandotte, Michigan - 1903
    Hull No.: 155
    Overall Dimensions: 436' x 50'3" x 28'3"
    Years in D. Sullivan Fleet: 1903-1911
    Official Number: U. S. 200376
    Other: Launched as WESTERN STAR. Renamed GLENISLA in 1918. Lengthened 72' in 1924. Renamed PRESCOTT (2) in 1926. Sold for scrap in 1962.

Steamer JAMES S. DUNHAM
    Built: West Bay City Shipbuilding Company, West Bay City, Michigan - 1906
    Hull No.: 620
    Overall Dimensions: 440' x 52'3" x 28'
    Years in D. Sullivan Fleet: 1906-1926
    Official Number: U. S. 203568
    Other: Launched as JAMES S. DUNHAM. Renamed LYNFORD E. GEER in 1926. Renamed OTTO M. REISS (2) in 1934. Sold for scrap in 1972.

Steamer W. E. FITZGERALD

Built: Detroit Shipbuilding Company, Wyandotte, Michigan - 1906
Hull No.: 167
Overall Dimensions: 440' x 52'3" x 28'6"
Years in D. Sullivan Fleet: 1906-1927 (as a bulk freighter)
Years in Gartland Fleet: 1928-1969 (as a self-unloader)
Official Number: U. S. 203561
Other: Launched as a bulk freighter. Converted to a self-unloader in 1928. Sold for scrap in 1971.

Steamer E. J. EARLING

Built: Superior Shipbuilding Company, Superior, Wisconsin - 1906
Hull No.: 514
Overall Dimensions: 555' x 55' x 31'
Years in D. Sullivan Fleet: 1907 only
Official Number: U. S. 203108
Other: Launched as E. J. EARLING. Renamed ROBERT B. WALLACE in 1924. Renamed PETER ROBERTSON (1) in 1957. Sold for scrap in 1969.

Steamer JOHN CRERAR

Built: Chicago Shipbuilding Company, Chicago, Illinois - 1903
Hull No.: 61
Overall Dimensions: 255' x 41' x 18'
Years in D. Sullivan Fleet: 1907-1916
Official Number: U. S. 200089
Other: Launched as the crane-equipped bulk freighter JOHN CRERAR. Renamed FOURAS in 1916. Renamed GLENGARNOC in 1922. Renamed COURTRIGHT in 1927. Converted to a tanker and renamed CEDARBRANCH (1) in 1940. Sold for off-lakes use in 1944 and scrapped in 1946 as EMPIRE NEWT.

Steamer H. G. DALTON

Built: Superior Shipbuilding Company, Superior, Wisconsin - 1903
Hull No.: 508
Overall Dimensions: 254' x 40'9" x 18'3"
Years in D. Sullivan Fleet: 1907-1916
Official Number: U. S. 96692
Other: Launched as the crane-equipped bulk freighter H. G. DALTON. Renamed COURSEULLES in 1916. Renamed GLENDOCHART in 1921. Renamed CHATSWORTH in 1927. Renamed BAYLEAF in 1942. Converted to a crane ship and renamed MANCOX in 1951. Sold for scrap in 1970.

Steamer A. D. DAVIDSON

Built: Detroit Shipbuilding Company, Wyandotte, Michigan - 1903
Hull No.: 153
Overall Dimensions: 252' x 41' x 18'8"
Years in D. Sullivan Fleet: 1907-1916
Official Number: U. S. 200185
Other: Sold for off-lakes use in 1916 and renamed ARROMANCHES. Sunk by torpedo from U-20 on October 23, 1916.

Steamer GEORGE C. HOWE

    Built: Chicago Shipbuilding Company, Chicago, Illinois - 1903
    Hull No.: 60
    Overall Dimensions: 250' x 41' x 18'
    Years in D. Sullivan Fleet: 1907-1916
    Official Number: U. S. 200000
    Other: Launched as the crane-equipped bulk freighter GEORGE C. HOWE. Renamed CABOURG in 1916. Renamed GLENEALY in 1922. Renamed CHAPLEAU in 1927. Sold for scrap in 1937.

Steamer J. S. KEEFE

    Built: Buffalo Dry Dock Company, Buffalo, New York - 1903
    Hull No.: 203
    Overall Dimensions: 254' x 40'9" x 18'
    Years in D. Sullivan Fleet: 1907-1916
    Official Number: U. S. 77580
    Other: Launched as J. S. KEEFE. Renamed PARAME in 1916. Renamed GLENFARN in 1921. Renamed CANMORE in 1927. Renamed ASHLEAF in 1942. Converted to a crane ship and renamed MANZZUTTI in 1951. Sold for scrap in 1970.

Steamer JOHN LAMBERT

    Built: Chicago Shipbuilding Company, Chicago, Illinois - 1903
    Hull No.: 59
    Overall Dimensions: 250' x 41' x 18'
    Years in D. Sullivan Fleet: 1907-1916
    Official Number: U. S. 77583
    Other: Launched as the bulk freighter JOHN LAMBERT. Converted to a crane-equipped bulk freighter in 1912. Sold for off-lakes use and renamed HOULGATE in 1916. Sunk by gunfire on November 22, 1916 23 miles southeast of Owers, Isle of Wight, England.

Steamer ALBERT M. MARSHALL

    Built: Detroit Shipbuilding Company, Wyandotte, Michigan - 1903
    Hull No.: 152
    Overall Dimensions: 255' x 41'2" x 18'9"
    Years in D. Sullivan Fleet: 1907-1916
    Official Number: U. S. 200091
    Other: Launched as ALBERT M. MARSHALL. Renamed BRIGNOGAN in 1921. Renamed FELLOWCRAFT (2) in 1929. Sold for scrap in 1952.

Steamer S. N. PARENT

    Built: Detroit Shipbuilding Company, Wyandotte, Michigan - 1903
    Hull No.: 151
    Overall Dimensions: 254'9" x 41' x 18'
    Years in D. Sullivan Fleet: 1907-1916
    Official Number: U. S. 117240
    Other: Launched as the crane-equipped bulk freighter S. N. PARENT. Renamed VEULETTES in 1916. Renamed GLENARM in 1921. Renamed CAMROSE in 1926. Renamed PALMLEAF in 1942. Renamed BLANCHE HINDMAN (1) in 1949. Renamed PARKDALE (1) in 1952. Deepened 5' in 1953. Sold for scrap in 1970.

Steamer JOHN SHARPLES

Built: Superior Shipbuilding Company, Superior, Wisconsin - 1903
Hull No.: 507
Overall Dimensions: 255' x 41' x 18'
Years in D. Sullivan Fleet: 1907-1911
Official Number: U. S. 77587
Other: Launched as the crane-equipped bulk freighter JOHN SHARPLES. Renamed CICOA in 1916. Converted to a bulk freighter in 1917. Renamed GLENVEGAN in 1923. Renamed WIARTON (1) in 1925. Renamed FLEETWOOD (2) in 1934. Sold for off-lakes use in 1944.

Steamer ROBERT WALLACE (2)

Built: Buffalo Dry Dock Company, Buffalo, New York - 1903
Hull No.: 204
Overall Dimensions: 254'9" x 41' x 18'
Years in D. Sullivan Fleet: 1907-1916
Official Number: U. S. 111466
Other: Launched as ROBERT WALLACE (2). Renamed TREGASTEL in 1916. Renamed GLENDOWAN in 1921. Renamed CHANDLER in 1926. Renamed ASPENLEAF in 1942. Renamed HELEN HINDMAN (1) in 1949. Renamed GROVEDALE (1) in 1952. Deepened 5' in 1953. Sold for scrap in 1959.

Steamer WILLIAM H. WOLF (2)

Built: American Ship Building Company, Lorain, Ohio - 1908
Hull No.: 360
Overall Dimensions: 524' x 54' x 30'
Years in D. Sullivan and Gartland Fleets: 1908-1966
Official Number: U. S. 205180
Other: Sold for scrap in 1966.

Steamer B. F. BERRY

Built: American Ship Building Company, Lorain, Ohio - 1908
Hull No.: 357
Overall Dimensions: 500' x 52' x 30'
Years in D. Sullivan Fleet: 1908 and 1909
Official Number: U. S. 204981
Other: Launched as B. F. BERRY. Renamed BERRYTON in 1922. Renamed VISCOUNT BENNETT in 1942. Renamed C. A. BENNETT in 1954. Sold for scrap in 1968.

Steamer MANCHESTER/JOSEPH W. SIMPSON

Built: Detroit Dry Dock Company, Wyandotte, Michigan - 1889
Hull No.: 91
Overall Dimensions: 256'9" x 42' x 23'3"
Years in D. Sullivan Fleet: 1908-1920 as MANCHESTER; 1921-1923 as JOSEPH W. SIMPSON
Official Number: U. S. 92087
Other: Launched as the bulk freighter MANCHESTER. Renamed JOSEPH W. SIMPSON in 1921. Shortened 41'1" in 1922. Converted to a crane vessel in 1928. Renamed MINDEMOYA in 1938. Renamed YANKCANUCK (1) in 1946. Sold for scrap in 1959.

Steamer CHARLES W. KOTCHER/ FRANK E. TAPLIN
> Built: American Ship Building Company, Lorain, Ohio - 1908
> Hull No.: 356
> Overall Dimensions: 440' x 52'3" x 28'6"
> Years in D. Sullivan Fleet: 1910-1915; in Gartland Fleet: 1950-1968
> Official Number: U. S. 204799
> Other: Launched as CHARLES W. KOTCHER. Renamed FRANK E. TAPLIN in 1920. Sold for scrap in 1968.

Steamer CHRISTOPHER
> Built: Superior Shipbuilding Company, Superior, Wisconsin - 1901
> Hull No.: 502
> Overall Dimensions: 414' x 48' x 28'
> Years in D. Sullivan Fleet: 1910-1923
> Official Number: U. S. 127583
> Other: Launched as the bulk freighter CHRISTOPHER. Renamed THOMAS BRITT (1) in1924. Renamed J. E. SAVAGE in 1928. Converted to a self-unloader in 1929. Renamed ROBERT J. PAISLEY (2) in 1932. Sold for scrap in 1969.

Steamer MERIDA
> Built: F. W. Wheeler & Company, West Bay City, Michigan - 1893
> Hull No.: 95
> Overall Dimensions: 376' x 45' x 26'
> Years in D. Sullivan Fleet: 1913-1915
> Official Number: U. S. 92514
> Other: Lost with all hands in heavy seas on Lake Erie on October 20, 1916.

Steamer MINNEKAHTA
> Built: F. W. Wheeler & Company, West Bay City, Michigan - 1893
> Hull No.: 93
> Overall Dimensions: 350' x 42' x 25'
> Years in D. Sullivan Fleet: 1913 only
> Official Number: U. S. 81427
> Other: Launched as the package freighter WILLIAM H. GRATWICK (2). Renamed MINNEKAHTA in 1911. Converted to a combination package freighter and bulk carrier in 1914. Lost when run on Menagerie Island, Lake Superior, November 1, 1924.

Steamer MINNETONKA
> Built: Cleveland Shipbuilding Company, Cleveland, Ohio - 1893
> Hull No.: 19
> Overall Dimensions: 342' x 42' x 23'9"
> Years in D. Sullivan Fleet: 1913 only
> Official Number: U. S. 107034
> Other: Launched as the bulk freighter ALVA. Converted to a package freighter and renamed MINNETONKA in 1911. Renamed GLENFINNAN in 1914. Renamed RENFREW in 1926. Sold for scrap in 1937.

Steamer MINNESOTA (2)
> Built: Detroit Dry Dock Company, Wyandotte, Michigan - 1888
> Hull No.: 84
> Overall Dimensions: 304' x 41' x 26'

128

Years in D. Sullivan Fleet: 1913-1915
Official Number: U. S. 95972
Other: Launched as the package freighter HARLEM. Converted to a bulk freighter in 1900. Converted to a combination passenger and package freighter and renamed MINNESOTA (2) in 1911. Sold for off-lakes use in 1917. Renamed FELICIANA in 1928 and scrapped under this name in 1931.

Steamer ROUMANIA

Built: James Davidson Shipyard, West Bay City, Michigan - 1887
Hull No.: 15
Overall Dimensions: 290' x 39' x 23'6"
Years in D. Sullivan Fleet: 1917 and 1918
Official Number: U. S. 110733
Other: Launched as a powered bulk freighter. Converted to a bulk freight barge in 1918. Abandoned in 1929.

Steamer VINDAL

Built: F. W. Wheeler & Company, West Bay City, Michigan - 1899
Hull No.: 127
Overall Dimensions: 240' x 40' x 16'3"
Years in D. Sullivan Fleet: 1921-1923
Official Number: U. S. 77362
Other: Launched as the bulk freighter JESSE SPAULDING. Renamed MOOREMACK in 1916. Renamed VINDAL in 1921. Renamed CORDOVA (1) in 1923. Converted to a self-unloading sandsucker and renamed JAY A. PEARSON in 1925. Renamed ROCKWOOD in 1935. Solf for scrap in 1963.

Steamer EDWARD U. DEMMER

Built: Detroit Shipbuilding Company, Wyandotte, Michigan - 1899
Hull No.: 133
Overall Dimensions: 440' x 50' x 28'
Years in D. Sullivan Fleet: 1922 and 1923
Official Number: U. S. 107523
Other: Launched as ADMIRAL. Renamed J. K. DIMMICK in 1913. Renamed EDWARD U. DEMMER in 1920. Sunk following collision with the Steamer SATURN (2) on Lake Huron on May 20, 1923.

Steamer MATHEW WILSON

Built: Quayle & Martin Shipyard, Cleveland, Ohio - 1872
Hull No.: None assigned
Overall Dimensions: 150' x 28'8" x 12'
Years in D. Sullivan Fleet: 1922-1926
Official Number: U. S. 120024
Other: Launched as FAYETTE. Renamed MATHEW WILSON in 1900. Scrapped in 1934.

Steamer O. E. PARKS

Built: James Elliot Shipyard, Saugatuck, Michigan - 1891
Hull No.: None assigned
Overall Dimensions: 140' x 28' x 11'
Years in D. Sullivan Fleet: 1922-1926
Official Number: U. S. 155208

Other: Launched as a powered bulk freighter. Converted to a bulk freight barge in 1928. Sunk May 3, 1929 off Thunder Bay Island, Lake Huron in a spring storm.

Steamer BENNINGTON (2)
Built: Chicago Shipbuilding Company, Chicago, Illinois - 1897
Hull No.: 28
Overall Dimensions: 255' x 42' x 26'1"
Years in D. Sullivan and Gartland Fleets: 1922-1944
Official Number: U. S. 116762
Other: Launched as the combination bulk and package freighter ST. PAUL (3). Renamed EDUARDO SALA in 1921. Renamed BENNINGTON (2) in 1922. Converted to a crane-equipped bulk freighter in 1929. Sold for off-lakes use in 1944. Scrapped in 1949.

Steamer BRANDON
Built: Detroit Shipbuilding Company, Wyandotte, Michigan - 1910
Hull No.: 183
Overall Dimensions: 252' x 43' x 26'6"
Years in D. Sullivan and Gartland Fleets: 1922-1944
Official Number: U. S. 207301
Other: Launched as a package freighter. Converted to a self-unloader in 1929. Sold for scrap in 1944.

Steamer BURLINGTON (2)
Built: Chicago Shipbuilding Company, Chicago, Illinois - 1897
Hull No.: 27
Overall Dimensions: 255' x 42' x 26'1"
Years in D. Sullivan and Gartland Fleets: 1922-1936
Official Number: U. S. 29769
Other: Launched as the package freighter MINNEAPOLIS. Renamed RAMON MARIMON in 1915. Renamed BURLINGTON (2) in 1922. Converted to a crane-equipped bulk freighter in 1929. Stranded and broke-up off Holland, Michigan on December 6, 1936.

Steamer ALEX B. UHRIG
Built: F. W. Wheeler & Company, West Bay City, Michigan - 1893
Hull No.: 100
Overall Dimensions: 378' x 45' x 27'
Years in D. Sullivan Fleet: 1923 only
Official Number: U. S. 126994
Other: Launched as the combination bulk and package freighter CENTURION. Converted to a bulk freighter in 1913. Renamed ALEX B. UHRIG in 1919. Converted to a combination bulk freighter and crane ship in 1927. Re-converted to a bulk freighter in 1931. Sold for scrap in 1946.

Steamer BACK BAY
Built: Great Lakes Engineering Works, Ecorse, Michigan - 1908
Hull No.: 36
Overall Dimensions: 256' x 43' x 26'6"
Years in D. Sullivan and Gartland Fleets: 1923-1944
Official Number: U. S. 204945
Other: Launched as the package freighter BURLINGTON (1). Renamed JUNEAU in 1915. Renamed BACK BAY in 1923. Converted to a crane-equipped bulk freighter in 1924. Sold for off-lakes use in 1944. Scrapped in 1950.

Steamer BROCKTON

Built: Great Lakes Engineering Works, Ecorse, Michigan - 1908

Hull No.: 37

Overall Dimensions: 256' x 43' x 26'6"

Years in D. Sullivan and Gartland Fleets: 1923-1944

Official Number: U. S. 204944

Other: Launched as the package freighter BENNINGTON (1). Renamed VALDEZ in 1915. Converted to a bulk freighter and renamed BROCKTON in 1923. Sold for off-lakes use in 1944. Scrapped in 1949.

Steamer OTTO M. REISS (1)/SULLIVAN BROTHERS (1)/HENRY R. PLATT, JR. (1)

Built: Chicago Shipbuilding Company, Chicago, Illinois - 1901

Hull No.: 50

Overall Dimensions: 450' x 50' x 28'8"

Years in D. Sullivan and Gartland Fleets: 1926-1933 as OTTO M. REISS (1); 1934-1957 as SULLIVAN BROTHERS (1); 1957 and 1958 as HENRY R. PLATT, JR. (1).

Official Number: U. S. 121208

Other: Launched as FREDERICK B. WELLS. Renamed OTTO M. REISS (1) in 1916. Renamed SULLIVAN BROTHERS (1) in 1934. Renamed HENRY R. PLATT, JR. (1) in 1957. Sold for use as storage grain barge and renamed PILLSBURY BARGE in 1959. Sold for scrap in1966.

Steamer ALABAMA

Built: Manitowoc Shipbuilding & Drydock Company, Manitowoc, Wisconsin - 1910

Overall Dimensions: 275' x 45'6" x 26'

Years in Gartland Fleet: 1933-1935

Official Number: U. S. 207138

Other: Sold for use in marine construction as a barge in 1964.

Steamer J. J. H. BROWN

Built: American Ship Building Company, Lorain, Ohio - 1908

Hull No.: 358

Overall Dimensions: 452' x 52' x 28'3"

Years in Gartland Fleet: 1935-1945 (under charter)

Official Number: 204993

Other: Sold for scrap in 1965.

Steamer JAMES E. McALPINE

Built: American Ship Building Company, Lorain, Ohio - 1908

Hull No.: 361

Overall Dimensions: 452' x 52' x 28'3"

Years in Gartland Fleet: 1935-1945 (under charter)

Official Number: U. S. 205076

Other: Launched as WILLIAM H. TRUESDALE. Renamed JAMES E. McALPINE in 1934. Sold for scrap in 1965.

Steamer RUFUS P. RANNEY (2)

Built: Superior Shipbuilding Company, Superior, Wisconsin - 1908

Hull No.: 520

Overall Dimensions: 440' x 52' x 28'6"

Years in Gartland Fleet: 1935-1945 (under charter)

Official Number: U. S. 205088

Other: Sold for scrap in 1960.

Motor Vessel ORMIDALE
    Built: Manitowoc Shipbuilding Company, Manitowoc, Wisconsin - 1917
    Hull No.: 81
    Overall Dimensions: 261' x 43'6" x 23'1"
    Years in Gartland Fleet: July-December 1935 (under charter)
    Official Number: U. S. 215702
    Other: Launched as the bulk freighter MOTOR I. Renamed LAKE MOHONK in 1918. Renamed
    ASTMAHCO III in 1920. Renamed ORMIDALE in 1922. Converted to a crane-equipped bulk
    freighter in 1934. Sold for off-lakes use and renamed JUPITER and BLUEFIELDS.
    Sunk off Atlantic Coast on July 17, 1942.

Steamer F. D. UNDERWOOD
    Built: Union Dry Dock Company, Buffalo, New York - 1896
    Hull No.: 78
    Overall Dimensions: 340' x 44' x 27'4"
    Years in Gartland Fleet: June-December 1936 (under charter)
    Official Number: U. S. 111123
    Other: Launched as the package freighter RAMAPO. Renamed F. D. UNDERWOOD in 1910.
    Converted to a crane vessel in 1930. Sold for scrap in 1940.

Steamer AMAZON
    Built: Chicago Shipbuilding Company, Chicago, Illinois - 1897
    Hull No.: 29
    Overall Dimensions: 390' x 46'2" x 26'
    Years in Gartland Fleet: 1944-1949
    Official Number: U. S. 30089
    Other: Launched as a barge. Converted to a powered bulk freighter in 1908. Sold for scrap in
    1953.

Steamer S. B. COOLIDGE
    Built: Chicago Shipbuilding Company, Chicago, Illinois - 1897
    Hull No.: 31
    Overall Dimensions: 396' x 48' x 26'
    Years in Gartland Fleet: 1944-1947
    Official Number: U. S. 30094
    Other: Launched as the barge AUSTRALIA. Converted to a powered bulk freighter in 1902.
    Renamed S. B. COOLIDGE in 1925. Sold for scrap in 1948.

Steamer COVALT
    Built: Great Lakes Engineering Works, Ecorse, Michigan - 1919
    Hull No.: 218
    Overall Dimensions: 261' x 43'6" x 27'6"
    Years in Gartland Fleet: 1944 only
    Official Number: U. S. 217774
    Other: Sold for off-lakes use in 1944. Renamed PATRICK SHERIDAN as a barge. Scrapped in
    1954.

Steamer JOSEPH WOOD/SULLIVAN BROTHERS (2)
    Built: American Shipbuilding Company, Lorain, Ohio - 1910
    Hull No.: 380
    Overall Dimensions: 524' x 54' x 30'
    Years in Gartland Fleet: 1953-1956 as JOSEPH WOOD; 1957-1967 as SULLIVAN BROTHERS
    (2).

Official Number: U. S. 207422
Other: Launched as JOSEPH WOOD. Renamed SULLIVAN BROTHERS (2) in 1957. Sold for scrap in 1967.

Steamer HENNEPIN (2)

Built: West Bay City Shipbuilding Company, West Bay City, Michigan - 1905
Hull No.: 614
Overall Dimensions: 524' x 54' x 30'3"
Years in Redland Fleet: 1956 as a bulk freighter; 1957-1969 as a self-unloader.
Official Number: U. S. 202088
Other: Launched as the bulk freighter SOCAPA. Renamed GEORGE G. BARNUM in 1915. Renamed HENNEPIN (2) in 1937. Converted to a self-unloader in 1957. Sold for scrap in 1975.

Steamer HENRY R. PLATT, JR. (2)

Built: American Ship Building Company, Lorain, Ohio - 1909
Hull No.: 370
Overall Dimensions: 524' x 54' x 30'
Years in Gartland Fleet: 1959-1969
Official Number: U. S. 206623
Other: Launched as G. A. TOMLINSON (1). Renamed HENRY R. PLATT, JR. (2) in 1959. Sold for scrap in 1970.

Steamer RALPH S. CAULKINS

Built: American Ship Building Company, Lorain, Ohio - 1902
Hull No.: 317
Overall Dimensions: 434' x 50' x 28'3"
Years in Gartland Fleet: 1959-1963
Official Number: U. S. 77532
Other: Launched as J. M. JENKS. Renamed R. R. RICHARDSON in 1916. Renamed RALPH S. CAULKINS in 1942. Sold for scrap in 1963.

Steamer EMORY L. FORD

Built: American Ship Building Company, Lorain, Ohio - 1916
Hull No.: 715
Overall Dimensions: 600' x 60' x 32'
Years in Gartland Fleet: August-December 1963 (under charter)
Official Number: U. S. 214318
Other: Launched as EMORY L. FORD. Renamed RAYMOND H. REISS in 1965. Sold for scrap in 1980.

Steamer CHICAGO TRADER

Built: American Ship Building Company, Lorain, Ohio - 1911
Hull No.: 391
Overall Dimensions: 545' x 58' x 31'
Years in Gartland Fleet: 1965-1969
Official Number: U. S. 209060
Other: Launched as THE HARVESTER. Renamed CHICAGO TRADER in 1965. Sold for scrap in 1977.

Steamer MERTON E. FARR
> Built: Detroit Shipbuilding Company, Wyandotte, Michigan - 1920
> Hull No.: 287
> Overall Dimensions: 600' x 60' x 32'
> Years in Gartland Fleet: 1965 only (under charter)
> Official Number: U. S. 220683
> Other: Launched as MERTON E. FARR. Renamed NIXON BERRY in 1966. Sold for scrap in 1970.

Steamer J. CLARE MILLER
> Built: American Ship Building Company, Lorain, Ohio - 1906
> Hull No.: 342
> Overall Dimensions: 545' x 55' x 31'
> Years in Gartland Fleet: 1965-1968 (under charter)
> Official Number: U. S. 202977
> Other: Launched as HARVEY D. GOULDER. Renamed J. CLARE MILLER in 1937. Sold for scrap in 1973.

Steamer NICOLET
> Built: Great Lakes Engineering Works, Ecorse, Michigan - 1905
> Hull No.: 9
> Overall Dimensions: 533' x 60' x 31'
> Years in Gartland Fleet: 1965-1969
> Official Number: U. S. 202542
> Other: Launched as the bulk freighter WILLIAM G. MATHER (1). Renamed J. H. SHEADLE (2) in 1925. Renamed H. L. GOBEILLE in 1955. Converted to a self-unloader and renamed NICOLET in 1965. Still in existence, though laid-up.

FARRAR TRANSPORTATION
COMPANY, LIMITED

The Farrar Transportation Company, Limited was organized August 28, 1903 in the Province of Ontario by Letters Patent. The incorporation was recorded on September 2nd by the Deputy Provincial Registrar showing the purpose of the action was "to buy, sell, own and operate, steamships, tugs, elevators, warehouses, tramways, wharves, docks and coal docks for freight and passenger business and to buy, sell, own and operate a wrecking plank." Capitalization of the company was established at $250,000, divided into 2,500 common shares of $100.00 par value each.

Mr. Charles Alphonzo Farrar was a native of Midland, Ontario, but he and his business associates established head operating offices for the company at nearby Collingwood, Ontario. In addition to Mr. Farrar, original directors of the firm were: Messrs. Francis Arnold Bassett, Francis Scott, Guildford Parliament Pearsall, George Edmondson Fair and William Carmichael. Letters Patent documents indicate that Messrs. Bassett, Scott and Pearsall were "Master Mariners" (captains), that Mr. Fair was a "merchant" and that Mr. Carmichael as a "capitalist." All were residents of Collingwood except Mr. Farrar. When the company acquired its two vessels, Captain Scott commanded the Steamer MEAFORD (1) and Captain Bassett was master of the Steamer COLLINGWOOD.

A misunderstanding between the intended owner of the Steamer NEWMOUNT, the Montreal Transportation Company, and the building shipyard led to Farrar Transportation acquiring its first vessel. In essence, Montreal Transportation backed away from the deal and the shipyard was left with a nearly completed vessel with no buyer. By this time, the new vessel had already been named NEWMOUNT. The name followed Montreal Transportation's common fleet suffix, MOUNT, and utilized the prefix NEW to indicate it was their new vessel. The carrier operated for its first season under that name, but was renamed MEAFORD (1) in 1906 in honor of Mr. Farrar's hometown.

The company's only other vessel was built for its account and was launched on October 5, 1907. It was named COLLINGWOOD in honor of the operating headquarters community.

The Steamer MEAFORD (1) was active in the Farrar Fleet until it was sold for off-lakes use during World War I in 1916. Its tenure on saltwater was fairly short, however, as it was sunk by a torpedo on June 11, 1917 while on a voyage from Gibraltar to Belfast, North Ireland with a cargo of phosphate rock onboard.

The Steamer COLLINGWOOD was equipped with a triple expansion engine which developed 1,200 shaft horsepower at 70 revolutions per minute. It also had two Scotch boilers with six furnaces. The boilers each carried 180 pounds per square inch of pressure. The vessel sustained three noted accidents during its service for Farrar. These were:

1. Summer - 1909:
The carrier stranded while maneuvering in Michipicoten Harbour, Ontario on the upper eastern shore of Lake Superior. Due to the very rocky shoreline and dredged channel, bottom plating and internal frames were torn and bent with repairs costing $12,094.65.

2. August 24, 1909
This accident occurred a little over a month after the Michipicoten Harbour mishap. The COLLINGWOOD was struck amidships by the Steamer GEORGE L. CRAIG and sunk in the Detroit River. She was raised on October 2nd and towed to the Detroit Shipbuilding Company at Wyandotte, Michigan for

repairs. These amounted to approximately $22,000. The vessel re-entered service in early November.

3. April 23, 1916:

      The COLLINGWOOD sustained bottom damage when it stranded in Whitefish Bay, Lake Superior during strong winds and current. It was released from the strand on September 25th and drydocked at Collingwood for repairs which ran to $5,688.72.

      Colors of the Farrar Fleet were: dark brown hulls with white cabins; the stack was a silvery white with a black band at the top and another black band about midway down the funnel.

      Mr. Farrar died in 1909 and fleet management fell upon the shoulders of George Fair. In 1912, headquarters were relocated to 107 Mail Building in Toronto, Ontario. Following sale of the Steamer MEAFORD (1) in 1916, the fleet was left with little flexibility. As events evolved during World War I, management decided to get out of the business and sold the Steamer COLLINGWOOD to Canada Steamship Lines on September 10, 1918.

      Farrar Transportation's last annual meeting was held on February 12, 1918. Upon sale of the COLLINGWOOD, winding-up affairs took precedence with management. Final corporate matters were concluded on December 31, 1919. At this time, officers of the company were: William E. Allen - president and George Fair - secretary and treasurer. Company directors at the close of business were: Messrs. W. E. Allen, G. E. Fair, D. D. Lewis, C. P. Pearsall, J. Shultis, M. Snetsinger and E. Stubbs. Surrender of the company's charter was accepted by The Honourable Harry Corwin Nixon on October 2, 1920 and recorded on October 13th in the Provincial Secretary's office in Toronto.

Steamer MEAFORD (1)

      As noted earlier, this vessel was renamed in 1906 for Mr. Farrar's hometown of Meaford, Ontario. It is located on Nottawasaga Bay at the southern tip of Georgian Bay, Lake Huron. The site was first settled in 1840 and for many years was an active port in Great Lakes shipping and shipbuilding.

Steamer COLLINGWOOD

      Collingwood, Ontario was named for Admiral Collingwood who was Nelson's second-in-command at Trafalgar. It was first settled in 1835 and saw its first industry in 1853 with the erection of a sawmill. For many years, it was the site of robust shipbuilding, but that company ceased operations in the mid-1980's.

Steamer NEWMOUNT at an upper lakes dock in 1906.

Steamer MEAFORD (1) at a Midland, Ontario coal dock in 1912.

Steamer COLLINGWOOD passing upbound in the St. Mary's River during the 1916 navigation season.

STATISTICAL AND OTHER PERTINENT INFORMATION FOR VESSELS OF THE FARRAR TRANSPORTATION COMPANY

Steamer NEWMOUNT/MEAFORD (1)

Built: Swan, Hunter & Wigham Richardson, Limited, Wallsend-on-Tyne, England - 1903

Hull No.: 292

Overall Dimensions: 259' x 42' x 20'6"

Years in Farrar Fleet: 1903-1906 as NEWMOUNT; 1906-1916 as MEAFORD (1)

Official Number: Brit. 118615

Other: Launched as NEWMOUNT. Renamed MEAFORD (1) in 1906. Lost when sunk in Atlantic Ocean June 11, 1917.

Steamer COLLINGWOOD

Built: Collingwood Shipbuilding Company Limited, Collingwood, Ontario - 1907

Hull No.: 17

Overall Dimensions: 406' x 50' x 28'

Years in Farrar Fleet: 1907-1918

Official Number: Can. 117089

Other: Launched as a bulk freighter. Converted to a package freighter in 1950. Sold for scrap in 1968.

THE WESTERN, WINNIPEG and BASSETT STEAMSHIP COMPANIES

All three of these distinct, but related steamship companies carried the same markings on their vessels. Black hulls were punctuated with white forecastles and cabins and the stacks were a solid black with a silver band encircling them near their tops.

The Western Steamship Company Limited was incorporated by Letters Patent in the Province of Ontario on January 30, 1903. It had a capitalization of $100,000, this being divided into 1,000 common shares with a par value of $100.00 each. The purpose of the firm's initial existence was "to engage in vessel agency and grain forwarding." Original directors of Western Steamship were: Captain William John Bassett and Messrs: Albert Eddleston Blackman, John Angus McKee and Donald Michael Waters. Headquarters of the firm was at 72 Bay Street in Toronto, Ontario where John A. McKee served as president and Captain Bassett served as the managing director.

The company flourished in its first four years and the officers decided to invest in a vessel of their own. They ordered a "canaller" in early 1908 from Swan, Hunter & Wigham Richardson's shipyard at Newcastle-on-Tyne, England and took delivery of the vessel in late summer of that year. The steel bulk freighter was christened JOHN A. McKEE.

The fleet grew to two vessels in 1909 when the Steamer WEXFORD was acquired from Captain W. J. Bassett. He had owned the ship personally from 1904 until this sale. He also sailed as the vessel's master from time to time. Unfortunately, the WEXFORD was one of those ships which met its demise just before the week of the "Great Storm of 1913." On November 8th, the steamer was enroute on Lake Huron with a cargo of steel rails when it was caught in a fierce storm and was sunk in the southern part of the lake. All twenty in the crew perished. The cargo was uninsured, but the vessel was insured in the amount of $107,300.

On November 1, 1912, Western Steamship entered into an arrangement whereby it would charter its Steamer J. A. McKEE to service the lake-borne transport needs of Algoma Steel and other industries in Sault Ste. Marie, Ontario. Western continued to manage and operate the McKEE during the period of this arrangement. Then, on February 24, 1914, an Agreement was entered into between Western Steamship and Algoma Central Terminals Limited whereby Terminals agreed to purchase sixty-four (64) shares of Western and also to purchase the McKEE for a total of $130,000, as follows: $65,000 in cash upon the McKEE's delivery to Terminals, $25,000 on February 24, 1915, $20,000 on February 24, 1916 and $20,000 on February 24, 1917. Interest was to be paid on the unpaid balance at the rate of 6% per annum. Instead of actually following this payment schedule, Terminals paid the discounted sum of $67,350.75 on September 22, 1914 and took title to the McKEE as of that date. Algoma Central Terminals Limited was a wholly-owned subsidiary of the Algoma Central & Hudson Bay Railway. The parent leased the McKEE to another subsidiary, Algoma Central Steamships, following closing of the above transaction.

It may be of interest to note from its commissioning, the McKEE was under the command of Captain Robert David Bassett, nephew of W. J. Bassett. Upon sale of the McKEE, the Western Steamship Company held its last annual meeting and the shareholders voted to wind-up the company's affairs. Mr. John A. McKee, of 218 Bay Street in Toronto, was then the chief officer in charge of liquidating the remaining assets of Western.

With the above move, Captain W. J. Bassett returned to sailing, but was semi-retired. His nephew organized the Bassett Steamship Company at this time as an unincorporated firm funded, in part, from some of the proceeds from liquidation of Western Steamship. The firm acquired the steel bulk freight Steamer MARISKA from the Pittsburgh Steamship Company on July 16, 1914 and operated it until September 13, 1918 when it was sold by Messrs. Stewart and Herdman, as brokers, to the Transatlantic Steamship Company for use on saltwater in behalf of Allied efforts during World War I.

Another unincorporated but affiliated firm of the two noted above was the Winnipeg Steamship Company whose principal was Mr. Eldon A. Woodward of Winnipeg, Manitoba. He acquired the steel bulk freight Steamer BRITON from the Pittsburgh Steamship Company on July 8, 1914 and operated the vessel the remainder of that season, then chartered it through a subsidiary, the Duluth Steamship Company, during 1915 with Captain C. A. Massey as master and Vincent Jarrett as chief engineer.

During 1916, the nominal operator was Duluth Shipping Company and, until the vessel's sale on October 29, 1917 for off-lakes use, the Massey Steamship Company, Inc., of Superior, Wisconsin was manager of the carrier on behalf of the Briton Steamship Company. The latter firm had been established by Captains J. Floyd Massey and C. A. Massey when they acquired Mr. Woodward's interest in the vessel. This pair also managed both the Duluth Steamship Company and Briton Steamship Company.

An additional note worth mentioning is that the Steamers GALE STAPLES and WESTERIAN have frequently been noted as having been chartered to Western Steamship Company. This is clearly incorrect since that company was out of business before the STAPLES took that name and the WESTERIAN was under other ownership when Western ceased operations. These two ships, therefore, are not indicated here to be part of the organizations which are the subject of this chapter.

Steamer J. A. McKEE

This vessel was equipped with a triple expansion engine and two Scotch boilers. It was named in honor of John Angus McKee, president of Western Steamship Company in 1908 when the vessel was constructed and delivered to that firm.

Steamer WEXFORD

Namesake of this bulk carrier was Wexford, Ireland at the mouth of the Slany River. It is seventy miles from the Irish capital of Dublin. While it formerly was a significant port, it is now superseded by the port of Rossclare to its east. The vessel was powered by a triple expansion engine and two Scotch boilers.

Steamer BRITON

The bulk freight Steamer BRITON was one of six staunch vessels built for the Menominee Transit Company in the early 1890's. The group was considered "the most modern" carriers of the time. After serving on saltwater during World War I, the BRITON returned to the Great Lakes and was employed in bulk trades for another decade. Its engine was one of the common triple expansion types and two Scotch boilers provided steam pressure. Namesake of the carrier was Great Britain's natives, but none specifically.

Steamer MARISKA

This steel bulk freighter was equipped with a triple expansion engine and two Scotch boilers. Its three cargo compartments were served by a total of nine hatches on the spar deck. Carrying capacity was 3,100 gross tons, making it about the same as the BRITON which had a capacity of 3,200 gross tons.

This vessel was originally part of the Minnesota Steamship Company. That firm utilized ship names which began with "M" and ended with "A." In this case, the namesake reference was to the Mariska River in Bulgaria.

Steamer J. A. McKEE downbound in the St. Clair River in Western Steamship colors in 1910.

Steamer WEXFORD downbound in Little Rapids Cut, St. Mary's River, in 1912.

142

Steamer BRITON downbound in Little Rapids Cut, St. Mary's River, in colors of the Winnipeg Steamship Company in 1916.

Steamer MARISKA passing downbound in Little Rapids Cut, St. Mary's River, in Bassett Steamship colors in 1918.

STATISTICAL AND OTHER PERTINENT INFORMATION FOR VESSELS OF THE WESTERN, WINNIPEG and BASSETT STEAMSHIP COMPANIES

Steamer J. A. McKEE

Built: Swan, Hunter & Wigham Richardson, Limited, Newcastle-on-Tyne, England - 1908

Hull No.: 798

Overall Dimensions: 259' x 42'10" x 25'

Years in Western Fleet: 1908-1914

Official Number: Brit. 125442

Other: Launched as J.A. McKEE. Renamed THORDOC (1) in 1927. Grounded in fog off Louisburg, Nova Scotia in April 1940 and was abandoned. Later broke-up and sank.

Steamer WEXFORD

Built: William Doxford & Sons Company, Sunderland, England - 1883

Hull No.: 145

Overall Dimensions: 257' x 40'1" x 16'7"

Years in Western Fleet: 1909-1913

Official Number: Brit. 87342

Other: Launched as WEXFORD. Renamed ELISE in 1890. Renamed WEXFORD again in 1894. Lost when sunk in severe storm on Lake Huron on November 8, 1913.

Steamer MARISKA

Built: Globe Iron Works, Cleveland, Ohio - 1890

Hull No.: 31

Overall Dimensions: 314' x 40'3" x 24'6"

Years in Bassett Fleet: 1914-1918

Official Number: Brit. 103979

Other: Launched as MARISKA. Cut in two for ocean service and rejoined in 1918. Cut in two for return to Great Lakes, rejoined and lengthened 48' and renamed KAMARIS in 1923. Renamed QUEDOC (1) in 1926. Sold for use as a barge in 1959. Sold for scrap in 1961.

Steamer BRITON

Built: Globe Iron Works, Cleveland, Ohio - 1891

Hull No.: 39

Overall Dimensions: 312'6" x 40' x 24'6"

Years in Winnipeg Fleet: 1914-1917

Official Number: U. S. 3493

Other: Cut in two for ocean service and rejoined in 1917. Cut in two for return to Great Lakes and rejoined in 1923. Wrecked upon stranding on Point Abino, Lake Erie on November 13, 1929. Broke-up in place November 21, 1929.

144

THE FOOTE TRANSIT, LAKE STEAMSHIP, TORONTO INSURANCE AND VESSEL AGENCY AND UNION TRANSIT COMPANY FLEETS

Many marine historians know this group of fleets by the names of Captain Foote and the Union Transit Company. They had their genesis uopn incorporation of the Toronto Insurance and Vessel Agency by Letters Patent in Ontario on May 31, 1910. This insurance and vessel agency latterly became known as Medland & Sons Agencies Limited, then M & W Holdings, Inc. before its dissolution when those Articles were filed on November 9, 1978. Over the years, various personalities connected with the Agency also became intimately involved in owning Great Lakes vessels.

Captain James Brown Foote was born April 4, 1875 in Owen Sound, Ontario and was educated locally. He began his sailing career on the lakes in 1891. According to his grand-nephew, he was known simply as "J.B." by most people who knew him. He rose up the ranks of the deck department and obtained his master's papers in 1896. He continued sailing until coming ashore in 1903 to take the position of marine superintendent of the Canadian Lake and Ocean Navigation Company Limited in Toronto, Ontario. This was a firm which was headed by Mr. James Henry Plummer and Sir Henry Mill Pellatt. In 1912, he left the firm to become manager of the marine department of the Toronto Insurance and Vessel Agency.

Letters Patent were filed November 14, 1922 on behalf of Captain Foote by Messrs. William Sargent Montgomery and Albert Mearns with Mr. Henry Corwin Nixon, the Provincial Secretary of Ontario. This action incorporated the Union Transit Company Limited. The new company's total authorized capitalization was $200,000.00 divided into 2,000 shares with a par value of $100.00 each. In actuality, however, only 300 of the shares were issued and paid for. Original shareholders and officers of Union Transit were: Captain James B. Foote-President & Director, George Richfield Donovan-Secretary/Treasurer and Director and Captain William John Bassett-Director. The former two were involved in the insurance agency while Captain Bassett was an outside director. He is also recognized in this volume for his involvement in the Western Steamship Company Limited prior to this time. Headquarters of Union Transit and the Agency were located at 64 King Street East in Toronto.

While the corporation had a perpetual life under its charter, in fact, it existed only until dissolution was declared by the Provincial Secretary on November 29, 1926. The last annual meeting had been held on February 20, 1925 when it was determined to file for a Dominion charter, and to do so in 1926.

Shortly after incorporation in 1922, Union Transit purchased the steel-hulled 'tween-decked package freight Steamer WAHCONDAH. This carrier remained in the fleet until its sale in 1925 to Abitibi Navigation Company Limited. The main reason for the sale was that the ship was not truly suited for the bulk trades of Union Transit, and when the company commissioned two new ships to be built and delivered, the WAHCONDAH was excess to the firm's needs.

The two new steel bulk freighters of 1925 were the Steamers JAMES B. FOOTE and D.B. HANNA. These were heady days at the company and a third ship was ordered and added in 1926. This was also a steel bulk freighter and it was named GEO. R. DONOVAN.

Ship colors of this fleet were black hulls with white cabins. Stack markings, however, differed during the years. In the earliest days, the stack was black with a white "T.I.V.A." monogram imposed upon it. In the later 1920's, the stacks were black with a white "U.T." lettered on the background.

Expanded operations and larger capital requirements for the three-vessel fleet were the underlying reasons for dissolution of the earlier firm and for its re-incorporation on December 1, 1926 under Dominion charter. The firm had authorized capital of one million dollars and named the same officers and directors as the previous concern with one major exception. That exception was Mr. David Blythe Hanna. He became an investor in the larger operation and took the position of vice president of the Agency. He was one of Canada's leading financiers at the time and had served as president of Canadian National Railways from 1918 until his retirement. He was born in Renfrew County, Scotland on December 20, 1858 and died in Toronto on December 1, 1938. Among his numerous directorships across Canada was that of Canada Steamship Lines.

The Agency was headed by Mr. William Schupp as executive vice president in 1926, with George Donovan serving as vice president, secretary and treasurer. Captain Foote was marine manager and actual president of Union Transit. It was through the Agency that the steel bulk freight Steamer WILLIAM SCHUPP was ordered and owned from its commissioning in 1928 through mid-1930 when its ownership was transferred to Union Transit Company. This was the same year that George Donovan was elected president of both Union Transit and the Agency.

During this time period there may have been some sort of internal upheaval involving Captain Foote. He was not identified with the Agency after 1926, having taken on the role of an independent insurance adjuster in 1927. In addition, he formed the Foote Transit Company Limited on February 23, 1929 with an authorized capital of $250,000.00. He was sole shareholder, but still shared space at 64 King Street, East. The stated purpose of this new company was "to own and operate the steel bulk freight Steamer F.V. MASSEY and to perform steamship agency activities."

Foote Transit colors showed a black hull with white cabins and a black stack with a large letter "F" imposed upon it.

With the Depression years came both unsettling times and another opportunity. Following the Mathews Steamship Company going into the hands of a Receiver in 1931 for default on its debt obligations, some of the vessels were put up for sale. Three of these were the steel bulk freighter Steamers BIRCHTON, CEDARTON and OAKTON. These vessels were purchased by the Lake Steamship Company Limited. Lake Steamship had been incorporated by Letters Patent under The Companies Act in Canada on December 14, 1922 with capitalization of $500,000.00. This was divided into 5,000 shares of common stock, each having a par value of $100.00. The company, however, laid dormant as far as vessel assets were concerned until it was used to acquire the three carriers noted above in 1931. All of the shareholders of Lake Steamship were partners in the Toronto Insurance and Vessel Agency.

When formed, Lake Steamship's headquarters were in Port Arthur, Ontario. They were re-located to 706 Canadian Pacific Railway Building in Toronto in 1931. The main office was moved into office space shared by the Foote Fleets in 1933.

Lake Steamship vessels carried black hulls and white cabins. The stacks were black on the bottom, followed by an orange band, a narrow black band, another orange band and a black top.

There was some disagreement among the shareholders of Lake Steamship about the future course of the business and, failing resolution of the discord, it was mutually agreed to dispose of all three ships and dissolve the company. This action occurred on December 13, 1937 when the vessels were sold to the Gulf and Lake Navigation Company Limited of Montreal, Quebec. The company charter was subsequently surrendered.

It is interesting to note that Captain Foote returned to the "fold of management" of Union Transit

Company in 1936. That year, Union's officers were as follows: Messrs. D. B. Hanna-President, G. R. Donovan-Vice President, and J. B. Foote-Manager.

On January 3, 1939, Union Transit sold its Steamers FOOTE, HANNA, and DONOVAN to N. M. Paterson and Sons Limited of Fort William, Ontario for $125,000.00 each. This move had the effect of covering asset value and reducing debt to zero. The remaining two vessels in the fleet. the SCHUPP in Union Transit and the MASSEY in Foote Transit, were operated through World War II, then sold to N. M. Paterson and Mohawk Navigation Company, respectively, in 1945 and 1946.

Mr. George Donovan, Sr. remained president of Union Transit through the sale of the SCHUPP, then retired. He died in Toronto on November 23, 1958. Captain Foote did likewise following sale of the MASSEY. He died July 28, 1951 after falling in his own bathtub and drowning at his home in Toronto. It was reported at the time that he died a happy man - "*with a cigar in one hand and a brandy in the other.*"

Steamer WAHCONDAH

The derivation of the name of this steel package freight carrier had its origin from the Sioux approximation for "great sacred spirit." The Sioux nation, like many other native peoples, used several names for the same thing, things or ideas.

During its several years in the fleet, this vessel is not known to have experienced any serious mishaps.

Steamer WAHCONDAH in Union Transit colors at Navy Pier, Chicago, Illinois in 1924

Steamer JAMES B. FOOTE

Captain James Brown Foote was the namesake of this steel bulk freighter when it was commissioned by the fleet in 1925. As noted earlier, he was president and a director of the Union Transit Company in 1925.

During the years of service in the fleets, the FOOTE is known to have sustained three mishaps which caused serious damage. These are:

1. November 6, 1928:
    On this date, the FOOTE grounded below Montreal, Quebec while upbound from Godbout, Quebec with a load of pulpwood in its holds and on deck. The ship was destined for Thorold, Ontario. The carrier was lightered and released November 8th, then reloaded for completion of the trip with temporary patching on the hull. The vessel was drydocked after being unloaded in Buffalo, New York where eighteen bottom plates were renewed at a cost of $10,468.89.

2. November 17, 1933, 0500 hours:
    While upbound with coal from Montreal to Toronto, the carrier stranded at a point 1,500 feet from the gas buoy on the east side of the channel abreast Wolfe Island, Lake Ontario. The stern was out of the water 16 inches as a result and the entire ship was aground from #1 hatch to the stern. Lightering was required with vessels from Kingston, Ontario. Following release, temporary patching and reloading, the FOOTE continued on her voyage. Later drydocking repairs were incurred in the amount of $19,380.20.

3. May 8, 1938, 1145 hours:
    While departing the Santa Fe Elevator on the South Branch of the Chicago River in Chicago, Illinois with a cargo of corn destined for delivery to Sorel, Quebec, the vessel's stern rubbed the dock on the opposite bank while in tow of the tug KANSAS which was turning the vessel around for the outbound trip up the river. The FOOTE lost its rudder plate, rudder stock and fractured its tiller. One propeller blade was also sheered off. The carrier was then towed to the South Chicago drydock of the American Ship Building Company for repairs after the cargo was unloaded at the Rock Island Elevator. Total cost of repairs and extra cargo handling amounted to $16,039.08.

Steamer JAMES B. FOOTE, upbound in Little Rapids Cut, St. Mary's River, in 1926
as managed by the Toronto Insurance & Vessel Agency for Union Transit Company

Steamer D. B. HANNA

Like the Steamer FOOTE, the D. B. HANNA was powered by a triple expansion engine and two Scotch boilers. Its namesake was Mr. David Blythe Hanna, Vice President of the insurance agency and president of Canadian National Railways in 1925 when his name was inscribed on this steel bulk freighter's bow.

During its tenure in this fleet, the HANNA is known to have suffered two serious accidents, as noted below:

1. September 19, 1934, 2300 hours:
    While upbound light from Montreal, Quebec to Cleveland, Ohio to load coal for delivery to Fort William, Ontario, the vessel struck the bottom of the channel in the Soulanges Canal. The grounding punctured #2 ballast tank and damaged internal framing. Pumps and temporary patching were able to allow the vessel to proceed to Port Arthur, Ontario for drydocking, bypassing the upbound coal cargo. Total cost of repairs amounted to $16,728.10.

2. November 28, 1937, 1950 hours:
    The HANNA was enroute, light from Port McNicol, Ontario to Fort William, Ontario. It left Port McNicol at 1710 hours in a strong southeast wind and rain. All went well until about 1825 hours when the wind swung to the northwest and blew violently with falling snow. At about 1840 hours, when near the Fairway Buoy off Adams Point, the visibility became very bad due to the falling snow. The wind had also increased in velocity to full gale force. The HANNA let go her starboard anchor at this time. About 1930 the anchor began to drag so the port anchor was dropped. As the wind increased to hurricane proportions, neither anchor was holding. The vessel increased her drift and eventually stranded on the north end of Osprey Shoal near the ranges in Georgian Bay, Lake Huron.

    Soundings determined leakage and distress signals were sounded and signal flags hoisted. At 1100 hours on the 29th, the nearby lightkeeper came to the ship in a small boat and was asked to relay a message to the ship's owner in Toronto about the situation. At about 1130 hours, the tug FANNY ARNOLD was nearby, but could not approach the HANNA due to the high seas. The tug, with Captain Foote onboard, reappeared on the 30th, and on December 1st, fastened a line to the HANNA which was effective in gaining release of the ship at about 1215 hours the same afternoon. Upon release from the strand, a survey was taken of the ship's condition. It was found that the rudder and shoe were badly damaged. The rudder was secured and the vessel was towed to Midland, Ontario, arriving there on December 2nd at 1600 hours. Further survey of the damage was made at this time and a decision was made to proceed to Collingwood, Ontario's shipyard to make permanent repairs. Fortunately, the Steamer ARLINGTON was in Midland at the time and performed the tow to the shipyard site, arriving there at 1220 hours on the 2nd. The surveyors report, signed by P. W. Wilson on behalf of the Salvage Association, attested to damage amounting to $48,162.58.

Steamer GEO. R. DONOVAN

Mr. George Richfield Donovan was vice president, secretary and treasurer of the insurance agency in 1926 when this steel bulk freighter took his name. The vessel was equipped with a triple expansion engine and two Scotch boilers. Its cargo carrying capacity was about 3,000 gross tons in its two cargo holds.

During its career in the fleet, the vessel encountered two recorded accidents of a major nature.

1. October 24, 1933, 0750 hours:

With a cargo of pulpwood from Godbout, Quebec to Waddington, New York, the vessel rubbed bottom on arriving at the channel going into Waddington. The site was near Clark Island. Bottom repairs were made later to the sum of $13,624.29.

2. August 31, 1934, 0525 hours:

With grain from Prescott, Ontario for Montreal, Quebec delivery, the vessel was in the vicinity of Sparrowhawk Point in the St. Lawrence River when it rubbed bottom heavily. Suspecting no damage, and finding no tanks leaking, the vessel proceeded on to Montreal. Upon unloading, further survey work was performed and a total of $15,737.10 was found in required repairs before further operation could be accepted by the underwriting authorities.

Steamer D. B. HANNA downbound in the Galops Canal in Union Transit Colors in 1927.
(Earl D. Simzer Collection/Courtesy of George Ayoub)

Steamer GEO. R. DONOVAN upbound in Little Rapids Cut, St. Mary's River, in Union Transit colors in 1930

Steamer WILLIAM SCHUPP

Mr. William Schupp, executive vice president of the Toronto Insurance and Vessel Agency, was the namesake of this steel bulk freighter when it took his name in 1928. The 3,000-ton carrier had two compartments in its cargo hold and these were served by seven hatches. A triple expansion engine and two Scotch boilers were installed in the engine room.

Three incidents of mishap are recorded for this vessel while serving in this fleet, as follows:

1. May 1, 1933, 0115 hours:

While proceeding upbound from Goderich, Ontario in the ballast condition, the vessel struck bottom in foggy weather and stranded on Cockburn Island Shoal, Lake Huron. The hull was holed, but pumps worked satisfactorily and were able to keep the vessel from sinking when released. She was towed to Collingwood Shipyards where repairs were made at a cost of $24,073.50. Upon completing this work, the vessel resumed its upbound trip to Fort William, Ontario.

2. September 18, 1936, 0755 hours:

The SCHUPP was upbound with a cargo of pig iron destined for Lackawanna, New York when it ran aground at the upper entrance to the Lachine Canal at Montreal, Quebec. The cargo had been loaded at Sorel, Quebec, about 35 miles to the east, so the trip had barely begun when the accident occurred. The vessel was towed off the strand by Sin-Mac Lines tugs and a temporary patch was affixed to the small holes in several bottom plates. Thereupon, the carrier proceeded on her upbound trip. Permanent repairs amounted to $8,789.62.

3. October 19, 1940, 1410 hours:

The vessel had departed Sydney, Nova Scotia on October 12th with a cargo of coal destined for delivery to Midland, Ontario. At the time noted, the ship was upbound in the Morrisburg Canal when it sheered to the port bank, then to the starboard bank, heavily rubbing both sides of the hull. Damage was done to both port and starboard plates and bilges. After temporary patches were put in place, the carrier was allowed to proceed, but only in daylight hours and only under tug escort on open waters. On November 13th, she was drydocked at Port Dalhousie, Ontario where permanent repairs were made. She was undocked on the 18th with repair costs running to $8,144.07.

Steamer WILLIAM SCHUPP in Union Transit colors, passing upbound in Little Rapids Cut, St. Mary's River, in 1936

Steamer F. V. MASSEY

Mr. Frederick Vernon Massey was manager of the Bank of Nova Scotia's branch in Toronto, Ontario when this vessel took his name in 1929. He was instrumental in helping Captain Foote and his associates with obtaining financing and was honored in this manner for that help.

The carrier was similarly equipped in its engine room as the SCHUPP, but had three cargo compartments instead of two in its hold. During its career in this fleet, the MASSEY is not known to have sustained any serious mishaps.

Steamer F. V. MASSEY in Foote Transit colors while moored at the R & P Coal Dock in Montreal, Quebec during the 1940 season

Steamer BRICHTON

Originally part of the Mathews Steamship Fleet, this carrier utilized that fleet's common name suffix, "TON" and specifically honored the birch tree as its namesake. Managers of the Lake Shipping Fleet did not see fit to change the name when they acquired the steel bulk freighter.

All three of the carriers in Lake Shipping were powered by triple expansion engines and were equipped with two Scotch boilers. Each had three compartments in the cargo hold and could carry 2,700 gross tons of cargo. No known accidents of a serious nature befell this vessel or its two sister ships while in Lake Shipping.

Steamer CEDARTON

Like the BIRCHTON, this vessel retained its original name and specifically honored the cedar tree.

Steamer OAKTON

As in the case of the two previous vessels, this steel bulk freighter kept its original name and honored the oak tree as its namesake.

Steamer BIRCHTON in Lake Shipping colors while downbound in Little Rapids Cut, St. Mary's River, in 1935

Steamer CEDARTON in 1936 at a newsprint unloading dock while in Lake Shipping's fleet

Steamer OAKTON in Lake Shipping colors while upbound in the St. Mary's River during the 1937 season

STATISTICAL AND OTHER PERTINENT INFORMATION FOR VESSELS OF THE FOOTE TRANSIT, LAKE STEAMSHIP, TORONTO INSURANCE AND VESSEL AGENCY AND UNION TRANSIT COMPANY FLEETS

Steamer WAHCONDAH

Built: Russell & Company, Port Glasgow, Scotland - 1903
Hull No.: 509
Overall Dimensions: 239' x 37' x 24'
Years in Union Transit Fleet: 1922-1925
Official Number: Can. 102577
Other: Sold for off-lakes use in 1955. Scrapped in 1968 as ALALC.

Steamer JAMES B. FOOTE

Built: Cammell, Laird & Company, Limited, Birkenhead, England - 1924
Hull No.: 903
Overall Dimensions: 261' x 43'2" x 20'
Years in Union Transit Fleet: 1925-1939
Official Number: Can. 147246
Other: Launched as EUGENE C. ROBERTS. Renamed JAMES B. FOOTE in 1925. Renamed PORTADOC (1) in 1939. Sunk May 7, 1941 by U-124 while enroute, in ballast, from St. Johns, New Brunswick to Freetown, Price Edward Island.

Steamer D. B. HANNA

Built: Furness Shipbuilding Company, Limited, Haverton-on-the-Tees, England - 1925
Hull No.: 91
Overall Dimensions: 261' x 43'2" x 22'8"
Years in Union Transit Fleet: 1925-1939
Official Number: Can. 147780
Other: Launched as D. B. HANNA. Renamed COLLINGDOC (1) in 1939. Sunk July 13, 1941 by enemy action, then raised, stripped and resunk at mouth of Scupa Flow, Scotland as part of an armada of scuttled vessels to form a breakwall for defence purposes.

Steamer GEO R. DONOVAN

Built: Furness Shipbuilding Company, Limited, Haverton Hill-on-Tees, England - 1926
Hull No.: 103
Overall Dimensions: 261' x 43'2" x 20'
Years in Union Transit Fleet: 1926-1939
Official Number: Can. 147782
Other: Launched as GEO. R. DONOVAN. Renamed KENORDOC (1) in 1939. Sunk by U-48 September 15, 1940 while enroute with timber on the Atlantic Ocean.

Steamer WILLIAM SCHUPP

Built: Furness Shipbuilding Company, Limited, Haverton Hill-on-Tees, England - 1928
Hull No.: 138
Overall Dimensions: 259' x 43'3" x 20'
Years in Toronto Insurance and Vessel Agency Fleet: 1928-1945
Official Number: Can. 160713
Other: Launched as WILLIAM SCHUPP. Renamed MONDOC (2) in 1945. Sold for scrap in 1961.

Steamer F. V. MASSEY
Built: Smith's Dock Company, Limited, South Bank-on-Tees, England - 1929
Hull No.: 873
Overall Dimensions: 259' x 43'9" x 20'6"
Years in Foote Transit Fleet: 1929-1946
Official Number: Can. 160720
Other: Sold for scrap in 1961.

Steamer BIRCHTON
Built: A. McMillan and Sons, Dumbarton, Scotland - 1924
Hull No.: 489
Overall Dimensions: 261' x 43'3" x 20'
Years in Lake Shipping Company Fleet: 1931-1937
Official Number: Can. 147893
Other: Deepened 2'6" in 1951. Sold for scrap in 1962.

Steamer CEDARTON
Built: A. McMillan and Sons, Dumbarton, Scotland - 1924
Hull No.: 488
Overall Dimensions: 261' x 43'3" x 20'
Years in Lake Shipping Company Fleet: 1931-1937
Official Number: Can. 147891
Other: Deepened 2'6" in 1951. Sold for scrap in 1962.

Steamer OAKTON
Built: A. McMillan and Sons, Dumbarton, Scotland - 1923
Hull No.: 487
Overall Dimensions: 261' x 43'3" x 17'6"
Years in Lake Shipping Company Fleet: 1931-1937
Official Number: Can. 147857
Other: Sunk September 7, 1942 by U-517 off the coast of Cape Gaspe in the Gulf of St. Lawrence.

VESSEL INDEX